PRINCESS

Diana

2020

PRINCESS *Diana* 2020

A QUEST FOR LOVE

WALTER OLEKSY

AuthorReputationPress®
Creativity & Branding

Author Reputation Press LLC
45 Dan Road Suite 36
Canton MA 02021
www.authorreputationpress.com
Hotline: 1(800) 220-7660
Fax: 1(855) 752-6001

Ordering Information:
Quantity sales. Special discounts are available on quantity purchases by corporations, associations, and others. For details, contact the publisher at the address above.

Printed in the United States of America.

ISBN-13:   Softcover   978-1-951727-22-2
                   eBook   978-1-951727-23-9

Library of Congress Control Number: 2019917493

CONTENTS

Part One 1

1. Prince Harry's Deepest Fear 3
2. Diana, We Hardly Knew You 7
3. Unwanted 10
4. The Engagement 13
5. Second Thoughts 17
6. The Wedding of a Century 20
7. Sex Life of a Princess 27
8. Charles's Television Interview 33
9. Margaret and Diana 35
10. Diana's Panorama Interview 37
11. Charles's Other Mistress 44
12. The Divorce 47
13. The Humanitarian 50

Part Two: The Men in Diana's Life 53

1. John Spencer, the 8th Earl Spencer 55
2. Charles, Prince of Wales 56
3. Prince Philip 61
4. Barry Mannakee 63
5. Bryan Adams 67
6. David Waterhouse 68
7. James Gilbey 69
8. James Hewitt 71
9. Oliver Hoare 75
10. Theodore Forstmann 77
11. John F. Kennedy, Jr. 78

12. Will Carling.. 79

13. Hasnat Khan 80

14. Dodi Fayed 85

15. Paul Burrell... 87

16. Ken Wharfe 90

17. Patrick Jephson 95

Part Three: The Inner Woman 97

1. Borderline Personality Disorder 99

2. Diana's True Love... 102

3. Diana and the Monarchy... 107

4. What Only Diana's Closest Friends Knew About Her 109

5. Conspiracy Theories 112

6. Diana's Funeral...119

7. Diana's "Secret Daughter".. 123

8. In Her Own Words... 126

9. Diana's "Pandora's Box" 129

10. Philip's Fatherly Advice 132

11. Diana and Mother Teresa...135

12. The Princess and the Queen 137

13. Diana and Astrology... 139

14. William and Harry..141

15. "The Best Mother" 143

16. In Diana's Footsteps... 144

17. This Above All...145

Works Consulted 149

About the Author.. 153

PART ONE

1

Prince Harry's Deepest Fear

The Princess Diana story lives on. It made front page news again as this was being written in October 2019. Her younger son Prince Harry revealed in an interview that he was still traumatized 22 years after her tragic death in a car crash in 1997 when he was 12 years old.

Harry revealed the emotional toll his mother's death has had on him. He admitted that his grief still was a "wound that festers." He told of his anxiety since her death during an 8-week trip he and his wife Meghan Markle took to Angola, Africa in the fall of 2019 to bring new attention to Diana's crusade against life-threatening landmines.

He said a great deal of his anxiety is caused by constant pressure from photographers and the tabloid media. "Every single time I hear a click, every camera flash, takes me straight back to the death of my mother. It is a wound that festers." He called the media's hounding of his mother a "ruthless campaign." Being followed by photographers himself is "the worst reminder of her life, as opposed to being the best."

Harry said that Meghan has been similarly hounded by photographers. "She is one of the latest victims of a British tabloid press that wages campaigns against individuals with no thought to the consequences."

The royal couple, the Duke and Duchess of Sussex, sued the London *Daily Mail* tabloid in October 2019 for publishing a private handwritten letter Meghan wrote to her estranged father, Thomas Markle, in the United States. She sent him the letter shortly after her 2018 marriage which he did not attend because of heart trouble, which may not have been true. Meghan was forced to issue an unprecedented statement confirming that her father would not be at the wedding. Prince Charles took her father's place and started walking the bride down the aisle. An independent spirit, Meghan left off holding his arm and walked most of the way solo.

Harry and Meghan charged the newspaper with misuse of private and personal information in breach of the United Kingdom's Data Protection Act of 2018. Further, they alleged that entire paragraphs of the letter were edited out so as to "manipulate readers" and fan the flames of a family feud.

A few days later, Prince Harry also reportedly planned to file a lawsuit against *The Sun* and the *Daily Mirror* tabloids and their parent company News Group Newspapers over alleged illegal interception of voicemail messages.

Love or unrequited love, which plagued Princess Diana her whole life, was reportedly behind the feud between Meghan and her father, as their relationship has been said to be strained for years.

In their defense, The *Mail* denied it erred by publishing the letter and said it did not delete parts of it.

The British press was divided about the merits of the lawsuit. While some newspapers have accused the Prince of being "sanctimonious" and "playing the victim card," others have defended the right of the royal couple to protect their privacy.

Prince Harry called publication of the private letter "internationally destructive." He said, "I lost my mother, and now I watch my wife falling victim to the same powerful forces of the tabloid media [*that had pursued his mother*]." He called it "ruthless, relentless propaganda." and said, "That has escalated over the course of her [*Meghan's*] pregnancy [*with their second child.*]

"I've seen what happens when someone I love is a [*commodity*] to the point that they are no longer treated or seen as a real person.

"I have been a silent witness to her [*Meghan's*] private suffering for too long. To stand back and do nothing would be contrary to everything we believe in. There comes a point when the only thing to do is to stand up to this behavior, because it destroys lives. Put simply, it is bullying, which scares and silences people. We all know this isn't acceptable, at any level. We won't and can't believe in a world where there is no accountability for this."

He said, "Any proceeds from the lawsuit will be donated to an anti-bullying charity."

Harry's older brother Prince William has similarly chastised the tabloid media and those who knew or worked for his mother and profited by their association with her. He said he felt that his mother was still being exploited for profit when Patrick Jephson's book, *Shadows of a Princess,* was published in 2000. His mother's former senior aide had betrayed her confidence in the book and profited by making public some of her private life.

Harry echoed his brother by saying, "There is a human cost to this relentless propaganda, specifically when it is knowingly false and malicious, and though we have continued to put on a brave face [*as his mother had*], I cannot describe how painful it has been."

William and Kate were no strangers to media invasion of privacy. When they vacationed at a private and secluded chateau in Provence, France, in September 2012, they mistakenly assumed they would have privacy from the paparazzi. But photographers found them and snapped photos of Kate topless while sunbathing, while her husband applied sunscreen on her butt. The royal family sued and a French court ordered the tabloid to pay Kate $120,000 in damages for invasion of privacy.

Harry said in 2019 that his mother's tragic death and the media's hounding of her has affected both his physical and mental health ever since, and he thinks about her every day.

While talking to Britain's daily newspaper *The Telegraph,* Harry said that he needed counseling in his late 20s.

"After losing mum at the age of 12, I shut down all my emotions for nearly 20 years and had been very close to a complete breakdown on numerous occasions.

"During those years I took up boxing, because everyone was saying boxing is good for you and it's a really good way of letting out aggression. And that really saved me because I was on the verge of punching someone, so being able to punch someone who had pads was certainly easier."

Expressing gratitude towards Prince William, Harry said that his older brother was a huge support to him and kept saying "This is not right, this is not normal, you need to talk to someone about all this stuff."

Harry added, "I can't encourage people enough to just have that conversation because you will be surprised firstly, how much support you get and secondly, how many people literally are longing for you to come out [*about mental illness which he may have inherited from his mother*]."

The Prince, however, said that he was a little nervous about the interview but he wanted to make a difference in the often hidden world of mental illness.

Prince Harry gave an extraordinary interview in 2019 in which he shared his anguish at having to walk behind his mother's coffin at her funeral procession. Harry had just turned 13 years old, a month before his mother's death, when he joined his father, Prince Charles, grandfather Prince Philip, 15-year-old brother Prince William, and uncle, Earl Spencer, in a funeral procession through the streets of London for his mother.

Speaking to *Newsweek* magazine, the Prince said: "My mother had just died, and I had to walk a long way behind her coffin, surrounded by thousands of people watching me, while millions more did on television. I don't think any child should be asked to do that, under any circumstances. I don't think it would happen today."

He said media hounding has escalated over the course of Meghan's pregnancy with their second child. Diana is dead. The British tabloid media can't hound her anymore. It may have found a substitute to hound in Princess Meghan.

Meghan told what it has been like the past year, navigating marriage, pregnancy, and new motherhood amid incessant media coverage of her life: "It has been really challenging. It has been a struggle. Look, any woman, especially when they're pregnant, you're really vulnerable."

Prince Harry said late in 2019, about the media's obsession with his wife, "My deepest fear is history repeating itself."

To lessen this possibility, the royal couple announced in late 2019 that they would take "family time" off and retreat from royal duties starting the middle of November. They did not say how long they would become virtually private citizens, but that it would be their lifestyle in 2020.

The night Princess Diana died, she told a friend that a retreat from public view and to enjoy a life of privacy was what she planned for herself.

2

Diana, We Hardly Knew You

Princess Diana's biographers so far have offered a jigsaw puzzle of who she was. But the pieces revealed only parts of her persona. This is an attempt to put all those pieces together, with the latest we know about her in 2020, so you can decide who she was.

The luckless Princess Diana got it wrong from the start. The Archbishop of Canterbury who presided over her marriage in St. Paul's Cathedral in London on July 29, 1981 asked "Will you, Diana Frances Spencer, take Charles Philip Arthur George as your lawfully-wedded husband?" The nervous and uncertain bride replied, "I will," but got the groom's names out of sequence, calling him "Philip Charles Arthur George."

Guests chuckled. That had the bride marrying the bridegroom's father. Diana's unintended blooper drew one of the few laughs in her 15-year marriage.

The venue for the marriage may also have been a jinx. Most British royal weddings down through the ages had taken place in Westminster Abbey. St. Paul's was chosen because it is larger and could hold more guests. It held one guest the bride wished she had not seen there. Quite likely, as she walked down the aisle to be married to the man she loved, seeing Camilla Parker Bowles, the woman who was her rival for his affections, made her nervous. Diana's nickname for Camilla was "The Rottweiler."

What really was "The Wedding of the Century" of Princess Diana and Prince Charles of England in 1981 that looked to millions of people around the world to be a fairy tale marriage? Diana later said, "It was the worst day of my life." Charles said, "My marriage was a Greek tragedy."

When Prince William, Duke of Cambridge and possible heir to the throne of Great Britain, announced in 2010 he was going to marry Kate Middleton, a British fashion executive, most every young woman in the world wished she was so lucky. One of them, American film actress Britney Spears, when asked if she would like to be in the bride-to-be's wedding shoes, replied that it was a no-brainer: "Who wouldn't want to be a princess?"

Diana Spencer, who had been married to William's father, Prince Charles, Duke of Wales, had said "Being a princess isn't all it's cracked up to be."

Diana had been there, done that. She knew from painful experience after 15 years of marriage to a man who never loved her, that the life of a princess can be far from what most women think or expect it to be. Being married to a man who loved someone else broke her heart.

We hardly knew luminous but enigmatic Diana before she died in a tragic automobile crash in 1997 at age 36. Many books have been written about her, but none have come close to revealing who she was, or what she wanted in the depths of her lonely heart.

Andrew Morton, one of the many writers who tried to understand who Diana was, wrote the 1992 tell-all book *Diana: Her True Story – In Her Own Words*. The book was written from audio tapes in which she privately told in intimate detail about her unhappy marriage to Prince Charles, his love for another woman, her own infidelities, and her difficult relationship with the Queen and others in the royal family.

Morton wrote, "In her life Diana was a complex web of contradictions: fearless yet frail, unloved [by her husband], but adored [by the people], needy but generous, self-obsessed yet selfless, inspirational yet despairing, demanding of advice but disliking criticism, intuitive yet unworldly, supremely sophisticated, yet constantly uncertain, and manipulative but naive.

"The woman behind the mask was not a flighty, skittish young thing, not a vision of saintly perfection. She was, however, a much quieter, introverted and private person than many would like to have believed.

"She could be willful, exasperating, a flawed perfectionist who would disarm with a self-deprecating witticism, her penetrating cornflower blue eyes seduced with a glance. Her language knew no boundaries; her lexicon [*means of communication*] was that of the smile, the caress, the hug and the kiss, not the statement of the speech. She was endlessly fascinating and will remain eternally enigmatic."

Diana was beloved by people all over the world. The compassion she showed the homeless, mentally ill, drug addicts, AIDS victims, and the sick and disabled – both young and old – earned her the title of "The People's Princess." But despite an adoring public, Diana spent much of her life feeling alone, unwanted, and unloved.

This writer, a former investigating reporter for *The Chicago Tribune* and the author of numerous books including biographies and histories, delves into the many mysteries of Diana, drawn from memoirs of the men and women who knew her best. Especially the men. Perhaps we learn more about who Diana was through knowing about the men in her love life.

We also report what no other biographer has revealed, that during his engagement and marriage to Diana, Prince Charles was in an affair with another woman besides Camilla Parker Bowles. So Diana had not only one rival for her husband's affections, but two.

Diana was a princess, but above all else she was a woman. We may come closest to knowing who she was by following the quest she was on her whole short life: to love and be loved.

Prince Charles, also growing up feeling unloved, was on a similar quest as Diana. Only after her death did he marry his true love.

3

Unwanted

Diana Frances Spencer was born on July 1, 1961 at Park House, the Spencer family's home. The mansion had once been a hunting lodge on the British royal family's estate near Sandringham, Norfolk, England. Her father, Lord John Spencer, a wealthy sheep farmer, rented the home from Queen Elizabeth II, whom he served as an aide. Her grandmother was the Queen's chief lady-in-waiting.

The third daughter of John and Frances Spencer, a noblewoman, Diana soon learned she had been born both unloved and unwanted. Before her birth, her mother had given birth to a boy. But he died ten hours after his birth, and John Spencer had wanted a son and heir to replace him, not another daughter. Diana felt her father's distance from her all her life. When Diana was three years old, her mother finally gave birth to a boy, Charles. He and Diana became close as children, closer than she was to her older sisters who were away at schools and they mainly got together on holidays.

Her parents were in a strained marriage since her mother was in love with another man. A family friend, Peter Janson, said her parents often quarreled, which greatly distressed Diana when she was a young girl.

Her mother left home after fourteen years of marriage when Diana was six year old. From up in a window, Diana watched her leave and drive off in a car after angrily slamming the door shut. The sound that made on a cold night remained with Diana the rest of her life.

Diana later recalled her mother's leaving. "The biggest disruption [*to my childhood*] was when Mummy decided to leg it [*leave*]. That's the vivid memory we have. It was a very painful experience."

Diana's parents divorced and her mother married a Scottish wallpaper heir, Peter Shand Kydd. They lived on his beef farm on an island in remote northwest Scotland some 450 miles from London. Diana's father was given custody of her and her siblings. They were then mainly reared by a succession of nannies, surrogate mothers whom they did not like. Diana saw her mother only on holidays.

Diana later said, "The divorce helped me to relate to anyone else who is upset in their family life. I understand it." She became determined that when she would marry, what had happened to her parents' marriage would never happen to hers.

Until the age of nine, Diana was educated at home by a governess. Her father then had her enrolled at a prep school, despite her pleading with him not to leave her there. She played the piano and was active in sports, but did not fit in with the other girls.

"I always felt different from everyone else [*at school*], very detached. I knew I was going somewhere different but had no idea where. [*I felt*] generally unhappy and being very detached from everybody else. At the age of fourteen, I just remember thinking that I wasn't very good at anything, that I was hopeless."

At a boarding school, West Heath, she was encouraged to become active in community service. It seemed to fulfill a need in her that remained the rest of her life.

Diana had an empathy for the lonely, because of her own lonely childhood, so she chose to visit the elderly. "I visited old people once a week, went to the local mental asylum once a week," she later said. "I adored that."

At this same time, she also developed an infatuation for young and handsome Prince Charles, although they never met. She saw his pictures in newspapers at society events or polo matches. She hung his photograph above her cot and told classmates, "I would love to be a dancer, or Princess of Wales."

Diana became a member of British royalty when she was 14 in 1975 when her grandfather John "Jack" Spencer died. Her father inherited his estate and title of the 8th Earl Spencer. She became known as Lady Diana Spencer and the family moved to Althorp, an ancestral family estate 75 miles northwest of London.

Diana's father remarried. Her stepmother was a divorcee, Raine Legge. She was a countess and daughter of romance novelist Barbara Cartland. Diana and her siblings resented her taking their father's attention and affection away from them. Diana said her stepmother was a "bully" who once threw her down the stairs.

Diana was very distressed that her father never told her or her siblings about his remarriage. She only learned about it from a newspaper article. When she confronted her father about it, she slapped his face.

Diana described her childhood as being "very unhappy, very unstable, the whole thing." She said in her secret videotapes, "My parents never loved me." They occasionally gave her a perfunctory kiss on the cheek, but never a hug.

4

The Engagement

Prince Charles in the flesh entered Diana's life when she was sixteen, in November 1977. She was attending a pheasant shooting party at Althorp when the guest of honor was the prince, who was then 28 and dating, among other young ladies, Diana's eldest sister, Sarah. Sarah was not in love with Charles and regarded him as an elder brother. She later said she would never marry Charles "if he were the dustman or the King of England."

Sarah introduced Diana to Charles in the middle of a field during the pheasant party. Diana regretted wearing corduroy pants, checkered shirt, and riding boots. Later, she recalled their meeting.

"I remember being a fat, pudgy, no makeup unsmart lady, but I made a lot of noise and he liked that, and he came up to me after dinner, and we had a big dance. .. He was charm himself... For someone like that to show you any attention... I was just so sort of amazed."

Prince Charles enjoyed meeting Diana that weekend, and she showing him how to tap dance. "What a jolly and amusing and attractive sixteen-year-old," he recalled. "I mean great fun... bouncy and full of life and everything."

Charles was a playboy and womanizer, but also looking for a wife. His mother the Queen was anxious that he settle down with a suitable wife who could give him an heir. His favorite uncle, Lord Mountbatten, also was encouraging him to put an end to sewing his wild oats and marry.

At the time of their first meeting in 1977, Charles thought Diana was too young to consider as a marriage prospect. Besides, he was not quite secretly in love with a divorced woman, Camilla Parker Bowles. They met at a mutual friend's house in 1970 and soon became close as they attended parties together and she frequented his polo matches.

Camilla had been married to Andrew Parker Bowles, a British Army officer, from 1973 to 1995 and had a son and daughter with him. Charles and Camilla resumed a relationship both before and during Charles' marriage to Diana, and after her death in 1997 they married in 2005.

His mother the Queen and the British government strongly objected to Charles marrying Camilla, encouraging him to marry a more suitable single virgin who could give him an heir. Meanwhile, Diana had fallen deeply in love with Charles, considering him to be Prince Charming to her Cinderella, although she was far from being a scullery maid.

Diana rocketed to the top of Charles' list of potential wives when they met again at a mutual friends' small house party in July 1980. He found her to be both beautiful and vivacious. Besides, she was an aristocrat, which would please his mother.

Charles and Diana rode beside each other on a bale of hay on a hay ride that day. He needed cheering up after the recent assassination of his uncle Lord Mountbatten, and was impressed by her comforting. Their first official date together soon followed as they attended a concert at royal Albert Hall. Her grandmother served as chaperon to the concert and a cold buffet summer afterward in his apartment in Buckingham Palace.

Charles then invited Diana to spend a weekend on his yacht during the annual August regatta. Within a month, he invited her to Balmoral, his mother's highland castle in Scotland. for the annual Braemer sporting games. Mindful that photographers were at the games and eager to photograph them together as a couple, while he was fishing she hid behind a tree, then walked away into a forest of pine trees.

Charles' courtship of Diana soon became worldwide front page newspaper fodder and everyone from Queen to commoner approved of their potential marriage. Except and despite Camilla.

On February 4, 1981, Charles invited Diana to dine with him in his apartment at the palace. Afterward, alone together in the nursery where he had played as a boy, he proposed to her.

Diana's reaction was, she was nervous. Her first reaction was to take his proposal lightheartedly. She giggled. Then she saw that he was serious, she accepted his proposal and told him she loved him. He is said to have replied, "Whatever 'in love' means."

"It wasn't a difficult decision," she said later, about marring Charles. "It was what I wanted."

After Charles' proposal, Diana went back to the London apartment she shared with three other young women when she was a kindergarten aide. She flopped down on her bed, and asked them, "Guess what?" Her friends replied, "He asked you!" She said, "He did, and I said 'Yes, please!'"

She showed off the engagement ring Charles had put on her finger. Someone [perhaps Charles] said it had been inspired by a brooch worn by his mother. It was an unique ring of oval Ceylon sapphire surrounded by 14 solitaire diamonds, all set in 18-carat white gold. In truth, it was not related to the Queen at all but she chose it from a tray of eight rings offered to her from Garrard, the crown jewelers. It wasn't even a custom creation. It had previously been featured in the jeweler's catalog for the American equivalent of $37,000. Diana reportedly chose it because it was the biggest ring on the tray.

One of her roommates remembered, seeing the ring, "We started to squeal with excitement. Then we burst into floods of tears."

Diana's son William slipped her engagement ring on Kate Middleton's finger when he proposed to her in 2010.

How William came to get the ring is a brotherly love story. Paul Burrell, Diana's butler and longtime friend, had known her since she was eighteen and became engaged to Charles. After her death, as temporary keeper of her jewelry, he asked her grieving sons what they might want of their mother's personal possessions, as something physical by which to remember her. William asked for her wristwatch. Harry asked for her engagement ring.

When William was to become engaged to Kate Middleton, he asked Harry if he could have the ring, to give to Kate when he proposed to her. Harry generously parted with his treasure. Not meaning to disparage William, Burrell said that it was just like Harry, who was more like his mother and had her generous heart. He said, "Harry has his mother's personality," a warmth with the people.

15

Diana told her roommate friends the night of her engagement to Charles that for the first time in her life, she felt secure. She was certain that she was going to marry without the fear her husband would leave her, and her marriage would not, like her parents', end in divorce.

Almost immediately after proposing to Diana, Charles suggested that they both may have been a little too hasty. He said she might need a little more time to consider the responsibilities she would be taking on as his wife and the likely future Queen of England. He suggested she might think over his proposal and give her answer again after she returned from a trip to Australia she had previously planned with her mother.

5

Second Thoughts

It could well have been because he was having second thoughts about his proposal. Had the bridegroom-to-be gotten cold feet. Was he already missing his life as a playboy? And, too, how would Camilla fit into his marriage? He did consider her to be the love of his life. Would he have to give her up? How could he do that? Maybe he wouldn't have to.

Over the nearly two weeks she was in Australia with her mother, Diana did not receive a single phone call nor wire from Charles. When she returned to London, there was no note from him. But she was still in love with him, and though only nineteen years old, she was confident that with his help, she could handle the duties of the Princess of Wales.

When she saw Charles again, she she accepted his marriage proposal a second time. She told reporters, "With Prince Charles beside me, I can't go wrong."

How did Charles feel about marrying Diana? Andrew Morton wrote that the prince told him, "Marriage is a much more important business than falling in love. I think one must concentrate on marriage being essentially a question of mutual love and respect for each other... Essentially, you must be good friends, and love, I'm sure, love will grow out of that friendship. I have a particular responsibility to ensure that I make the right decision. The last thing I could possibly entertain is getting divorced."

How did Diana feel about marrying Prince Charles? Penny Junor wrote in her book *Diana, Princess of Wales,* Diana said, " A woman not only marries a man; she marries into a way of life... a job. She's got to have some knowledge of it; some sense of it; otherwise she wouldn't have a clue about whether she's going to like it. If I'm deciding on whom I want to live with for fifty years, well that's the last decision on which I want my head to be ruled by my heart. To me, marriage seems to be the biggest and most responsible step to be taken in one's life."

The royal engagement made news around the world. The union would become the wedding of the century. While most people believed Charles and Diana were meant for each other, some had their doubts. In their likes and dislikes, were they actually opposites? He liked to read philosophical books, while she preferred romance novels. He liked opera and classical music while she liked ballet and rock and roll. Charles loved the country and simple outdoor pleasures such as gardening, while Diana preferred the city life with its parties and dances.

More importantly, their views on love were different. During an interview announcing their engagement, a television reporter asked them whether they were in love. "Of course!" Diana said, smiling shyly. Charles said, "Whatever 'in love' means," repeating the words he had said after proposing to her. Diana was visibly disappointed by his remark.

While Diana loved Charles completely, he apparently was unsure about his feelings for her. In some ways, she was the right woman for him. In his heart, she was not.

Charles confided in a friend, "I expect it will be the right thing in the end. I do very much want to do the right thing for this country and for my family. But I'm terrified sometimes at making a promise and then perhaps living to regret it."

Two weeks before his marriage to Diana, she learned that Charles had given Camilla a bracelet with the initials *G* and *F* twined in it. She then learned that the initials stood for Gladys and Fred, which were Camilla's and Charles' secret pet names for each other.

It upset Diana so much, she told her sisters, "I can't marry him. I can't do this. This is absolutely unbelievable." They replied, "Well, bad luck, Duch... You're too late to chicken out." Duch, short for Duchess, was Diana's sisters pet name for her.

At the rehearsal three days before her wedding, Diana tried to forget her broken heart. She later recalled, "I remember being so much in love with my [future] husband that I couldn't take my eyes off of him. I just thought I was the luckiest girl in the world. He was going to look after me. Well, I was wrong on that assumption."

Camilla even phoned Charles at Buckingham Palace. Diana and Charles were in the study, she preparing for the wedding and he for trips to Australia and New Zealand in the weeks before the wedding. The phone rang and Diana answered it. She recognized it was Camilla calling, asking to speak to Charles.

Diana later said she wondered, "Shall I be nice or sit here? I thought I'd be nice so I left them to it [to say goodbye to each other while he would be away]. It just broke my heart." They were not even married yet, and he was being unfaithful.

Sally Bedell Smith wrote in her 1999 book *Prince Charles: The Passions and Paradoxes of an Improbable Life*, that Charles and Diana were both deeply unhappy, or at least she was, literally from Day One of their marriage. Regarding Charles, she said "Going into something like [the marriage], I think he felt it was for life. He wasn't sure about the relationship, and I think he felt incredibly trapped, probably, on the eve of his wedding."

Diana said about her wedding, "I don't think I was happy. The Camilla thing rearing its head the whole way through our engagement... I was desperately trying to be mature about the situation, but I didn't have the foundation to do it, and I couldn't talk to anyone about it. I realized I had taken on an enormous role, but had no idea what I was going into. But no idea."

6

The Wedding of a Century

In her wedding vows, Diana did not say she would obey him. Instead, she promised "to love him, comfort him, and keep him in sickness and health."

At the ceremony, when the Archbishop of Canterbury asked the bride if she would marry the man standing with her, Diana could not remember all his first names, and spoke them wrong.

Something else was wrong at the wedding. The bride and groom were of the same height, a tall 5 feet, 10 inches. But Charles always wore some kind of "elevator shoes" that made him look a foot taller than Diana. He rose to the wedding occasion wearing military horseman's riding boots. They were not patent leather.

During her engagement, Diana didn't think much of Charles's clothes. His suits were both baggy and boring. She particularly did not like the flannel pajamas he wore to their bed. Among her wedding gifts to him were some silk pajamas. Diana's wedding dress had the longest train anyone had ever seen. The media covered the bride in great detail. Only her under garments were not described.

What became called The Wedding of the Century, watched by millions of people on television all over the world, the most watched event in human history began on a hopeful note. That came in the form of a note Charles sent to Diana the night before they wed in St. Paul's Cathedral in London on July 29, 1981. The note read, "I'm so proud of you, and when you come up [*the aisle*] I'll be there at the altar for you tomorrow. Just look 'em in the eye and knock 'em dead."

They were the first words of encouragement she ever got from him, and apparently the last. At other times during their engagement and especially during their marriage, he criticized her so that she lost confidence in herself.

Diana did knock them dead the next morning, when as her brother later said, she looked radiant, happy, composed, and calm. But her eyes also would be on the 2,500 guests attending in the cathedral, as she looked to see if Camilla Parker Bowles was among them. She was, and as Diana walked down the aisle in a gorgeous veiled ivory silk taffeta wedding gown on the arm of her father, who was weak after suffering a near-fatal stroke just weeks earlier, she saw her.

As Diana told Andrew Morton some years later, "I knew she was there. Walking down the aisle, I spotted Camilla [*wearing a*] pale gray veiled pillbox hat, her [*young*] son Tom standing [*on the church bench beside her*]."

Maybe now Diana's father was glad his wife had given birth to a third daughter instead of a son. He was a proud father at her wedding to the potential future king of England, but never was the loving father Diana wanted. Now she hoped she was going to find a loving husband.

In that regard, Charles was off to a bad start. After the Archbishop of Canterbury pronounced them man and wife, traditionally at weddings the groom then kissed his bride. But Charles, militarily dressed in his uniform as commanding officer of the Household Cavalry Mounted Regiment, did not follow tradition. He did not kiss Diana.

That came later, and only in a way. After they rode to Buckingham Palace in a horse-drawn glass coach and greeted the thousands who cheered them from outside. Appearing on the balcony, Diana whispered to her husband, "They want us to kiss." He replied nonchalantly, "Why not?"

But he then showed no sign of being about to kiss her, so she kissed him. To Diana, it was not the same as him kissing her, but from a distance the cheering crowds couldn't tell.

The newlyweds honeymooned aboard the royal yacht including a twelve-day cruise through the Mediterranean to Egypt. Upon their return, they took up residence in an apartment at Buckingham Palace. It held a master bedroom suite, living room, two guest rooms, a nursery, servants rooms, and three reception rooms. No rent, of course.

Diana immediately went to work as the Princess of Wales. She had expected to be well-trained for the role, but in truth, according to her biographers, got perhaps even less training than a clerk in a department store. Despite this, she accompanied the Prince at official royal events including dinners for visiting dignitaries and cutting ribbons for occasions such as ceremonial tree plantings. She was always obliged to wear a hat when in public and walk behind her husband, never ahead of him.

She soon became a darling of fashion designers and was constantly photographed wearing the latest clothes. Even her hair style was front-page news and copied as "the Princess Diana haircut." Charles soon became jealous as she became more popular with the public.

As photographers and news reporters followed her every move outside the palace, Diana began to feel the pressures of being a public figure. She realized early that she had lost her private life.

One of Charles' private secretaries later wrote, about this pressure: "Almost any human being would have found it absolutely intolerable. Wherever [*Diana*] happened to be, every look, every gaze, every smile, every scowl. every hand [she] held or touched [*was*] under the microscope, every time front page news in the tabloids day after day. Everybody after [*her.*] [*She was*] under the most extraordinary pressure."

Meanwhile, Prince Charles was under pressures of his own, despite being reared to expect them. Marriage had required him to give up many of his friends and aides, as well as Camilla.

He even gave up his dog, a big yellow Labrador Retriever named Harvey whom he had taken on foreign trips and hunting outings. Diana had insisted he give up Harvey because she associated the dog with his bachelor past. Reluctantly, he gave Harvey to an aide.

Media attention grew even stronger on Diana when she was expecting her first child with Charles. She apparently had not fully understood the lack of privacy she would face by becoming Charles' wife and England's Princess Di.

James Whitaker, the London *Mirror's* royalty reporter, said. "She didn't know she was marrying us as well."

In June 1982, Diana had been in a depressed state about Camilla while being four months pregnant and, while living with Charles in his house at Highgrove, intentionally threw herself down a flight of stairs. However, the pregnancy continued and her son William was born healthy on June 21.

In another suicide attempt, during her honeymoon at Balmoral, Diana said, "I picked up [Charles's] penknife off his dressing table and scratched myself heavily down my chest and both thighs. There was a lot of blood. And he [Charles] hadn't made any reaction whatsoever."

Two years later Diana gave birth to Henry, known as Harry, on September 15, 1984. The brothers became known as "the heir and the spare."

Diana must have had a feeling of *deje vu* at Harry's birth. She later said that Charles had wanted their second child to be a girl. Perhaps that would avoid any dispute between them later, as to which one should become king.

Diana said that just after she had given birth to Harry, Charles remarked with mild disappointment, "Oh God, it's a boy! " and went off to play polo.

Charles wanted the boys to be reared by nannies, as he had been. Although he wouldn't admit it, he had grown up longing for the care of a loving mother. The Queen was not that. She was busy focused on being Queen.

Paul Burrell, the royal couple's butler at Highgate, said years later, "[*The trouble with Charles was*] He never wanted a lover; he wanted a mother." The Queen did not give him the motherly love he longed for.

Diana had not liked being brought up by nannies and not a loving mother. She wanted their sons to be reared like normal boys, so she insisted she be allowed to spend as much time with them as her public duties permitted. She became a loving, even a doting, mother.

Charles agreed, but Diana's ever-growing popularity from visiting the sick and elderly in hospitals made him increasingly jealous of the attention she was getting in the tabloids. As he told a friend, "It's only Diana they [*the media*] want now. I don't count anymore."

He was right. Media coverage of Diana even intensified when she began becoming a humanitarian. The press followed as she visited hospitals with the elderly and those suffering from drug addition or AIDS. She later said, "I found myself being more and more involved with people who were rejected by society... and I found an affinity there."

There were really two very different sides to Diana. There was the public side that in which people wanted a fairy tale princess. If she touched them, all their worries would go away. They didn't know her private side, hidden inside because she didn't think she was good enough.

She did not feel she belonged as a member of the royal Family. She said, "When I first arrived on the royal scene, I was just so frightened of the attention I was getting... It was too much for one person at that time.

"I didn't want to do anything on my own, I was too frightened . The thought of me doing anything on my own sent tremors, so I stuck with whatever Charles, did."

She found it difficult to adjust to the royal routine at Buckingham Palace, Windsor Castle, and at Balmoral, the Queen's residence in Scotland. She felt very alone. "No one talks to me. I feel totally out of place. I sometimes wonder what on earth I've gotten myself into. I feel so small, so lonely, so out of my depth. All I can talk about is the bloody weather!

"No one ever talks to me [at social events.] I stand around at every official gathering not to know what to do, what to say, or where to look. I'm worried that I might do something wrong, and I feel like a fish out of water."

Above all, there was her relationship with Charles' mother, Queen Elizabeth II.

"I'm absolutely petrified of the Queen. I shake all over when I'm in her presence. I can't look her in the eye, and just go to pieces whenever she comes into the room. She tries to be nice, and put me at my ease, but I am so embarrassed when I am with her."

At the same time, Charles' true love continued to haunt Diana's marriage. Camilla Parker Bowles and Charles remained close friends after they both married other people. He had been willing to give up his dog, but not his not-so-secret paramour.

It was like a bad television soap opera as Camilla became a frequent visitor to Charles' home at Highgrove where she hosted his lunches and dinners and virtually ran his house while Diana was in London.

Charles' butler., Paul Durrell, saw Camilla often at Highgrove but when Diana would call asking what Charles was doing, he covered for him.

In 1991, Diana remained at their home in London while Charles went on a week-long holiday visiting art galleries and museums in Italy. Camilla joined him there.

After the royal couple divorced, Diana said in an interview, that she and Charles "had discussions about Camilla. I once heard him on the telephone in his bath and saying [to Camilla] 'Whatever happens, I will always love you.' I told him afterwards that I had listened at the door, and we had a filthy row [*about it*]."

Diana felt helpless about the situation. "I wasn't in a position to do anything about it," she said, because her husband was the future King of England, and she could not help the fact he was still in love with Camilla.

Stressful feelings from the situation caused Diana to have severe eating problems. She had been struggling a long time with an eating disorder called bulimia, or compulsive over-eating. When stressed, she would make herself sick by over-eating. Then she would throw up the food so she would not gain weight. She did this sometimes four or five times a day, depending on how stressed-out she was.

She revealed in an interview, "I had bulimia for a number of years. It's like a secret disease... You inflict it upon yourself because your self esteem is at a low ebb and you don't think you're worthy or of value. You fill your stomach up four or five times a day. Some do it more, and it gives you a feeling of comfort."

Diana said her bulimia "began the week we got engaged. My [future] husband put his hand on my waistline and said, 'Oh, a bit chubby here, aren't we?' That triggered off something in me."

Diana's eating troubles plagued her on her honeymoon. Aboard the royal yacht *Britannia*, she would creep into the galley, or kitchen, at odd hours to consume large bowls of ice cream and other sweets.

"By then the bulimia was appalling," she recalled. It was rife, four times a day on the yacht. Anything I could find I would gobble up and be sick two minutes later, [*feeling*] very tired. So, of course that got the mood swings going in the sense that one minute one would be happy, next blubbering one's eyes out."

"They were desperate cries for help," Diana says in *Her True Story*. "I just needed time to adjust to my new position.

One friend who watched their relationship deteriorate pointed to Prince Charles's disinterest and total lack of respect for her at a time when Diana badly needed help.

"His indifference pushed her to the edge whereas he could have romanced her to the end of the world. They could have set the world alight. Through no fault of his own, because of his own ignorance, upbringing and lack of a whole relationship with anyone in his life, he instilled this hatred of herself."

Charles had not assured his bride that he would be there for her. She counted on that, but he wasn't. Diana's sense of duty and a determination not to fail and let down the public guided her through her marriage.

7

Sex Life of a Princess

Diana's eating disorder continued throughout her marriage. She wrote after her divorce that the bulimia was not only caused by Camilla stress. She believed it went back to childhood memories of feeling unwanted because she had been born a girl instead of a boy, which her father had wanted. Also the trauma of her parents' divorce, anxiety of being the wife of the future king, and constant attention from the media.

Most of all, Diana believed the bulimia came from a lack of self-esteem that was magnified by not feeling wanted or loved by her husband and, as she later said, "that Camilla thing. I was desperate. Desperate."

Diana found some relief from "the Camilla thing" by finding affection apart from and probably in spite of her husband. As he was not faithful to her, she played a tit-for-tat game and was not faithful to him. She began relationships with two handsome bachelors.

First, in 1986, five years into her loveless marriage, Diana began a two-year relationship with a London banker which lasted until he married. A thorough search does not bring up his name or details of their affair.

Another relationship followed a year later. She and a major in the Household Cavalry became close as he escorted her to disco dances and rock concerts that Charles had no interest in.

A much more serious relationship began in 1991 with British Army Major James Hewitt who gave her riding lessons.

Diana was photographed extensively in these relationships, especially with Hewitt, and the photos appeared on the front pages of London tabloids. Charles saw them but did not confront her about them.

Besides these men, Diana's closet friends early in her marriage were her former apartment roommates and Sarah "Fergie" Ferguson, daughter of Prince Charles' polo master who became Prince Andrew's wife. Prince Andrew, the Duke of York, was the second son of Queen Elizabeth II and Prince Phillip.

Fergie worked in a London art house and she and Andrew also had an apartment in Buckingham Palace while Diana and Charles lived there for a time after their marriage. Neither Charles nor the Queen approved of Fergie or her marriage in 1986 which ended after just five years in 1992.

Diana and Fergie had some good times together, of which Charles disapproved. The two women had several things in common. Like Diana's parents, Fergie's also had divorced, when she was thirteen. Her mother had walked out on her marriage, as Diana's mother had, so they shared childhood traumas.

They also enjoyed playing pranks. On one occasion, they attempted to crash Andrew's bachelor party by disguising themselves as uniformed policewomen. When they were found out and turned away, they wore their uniforms to a fashionable nightclub.

Charles reprimanded Diana for "trashing the dignity of the royal family." She chided him for being "stuffy, boring, and old before his time."

In some private taped interviews with her speech coach Peter Settleten between 1992 and 1993,, Diana revealed what her sex life was like married to Charles. The tapes were made after she and Charles had been married 12 years and had had their sons.

"Well, there was [sex]," she said. "There was. There was. But it was odd, very odd. It was there, then it fizzled out, about seven years ago, six years ago, well seven, because Harry was eight.

"Instinct told me, it was just so odd. I don't know, there was no requirement for it from his case. Sort of once every three weeks. And then it followed a pattern... He used to see his lady [*Camilla*] once every three weeks before we got married.

"He wasn't consistent with his courting abilities [*during their engagement*]. He'd ring me up every day for a week, then he wouldn't speak to me for three weeks. Very odd. And I accepted that and I thought fine, he knows where I am if he wants me. And then the thrill when he used to ring up was so immense and intense, drive the other three girls in my flat crazy. But no, it was all, it was odd."

Diana said that once during their engagement, "He leaped upon me, he started kissing me and everything, and I thought, this is not what people do, and he was all over me for the rest of the evening, followed me around like a puppy. I was flattered, but it was very puzzling."

Diana and Charles' marriage began to fail as soon as it had begun. As a British ambassador said, "It is sad, but it was all wrong from the very beginning. To Diana, Charles was a fantasy figure with whom she was besotted [*infatuated*]. To Charles, Diana was the young bride who would become the perfect princess, always at his side and willing to fall in with his wishes and his lifestyle."

Penny Junor, Diana's biographer, agreed, writing that "There was never any depth to their understanding of each other. Diana could not become the soulmate he wanted in a wife [*Camilla was already that.*] She didn't share his enthusiasm for books or horses or gardening, or opera or the dozens of things which she had pretended to be so interested in at the onset. She was not the one to cure the loneliness and uncertainty of his life, or to give him the unconditioned love and support and reassurance he needed to make him a confident and happy man... because she desperately needed all of these things herself."

Another observer of the royal couple said about their breakup: "The problems of the marriage have come out in the open because Di's self-confidence has developed. She now appreciates her own incredible sexuality and the fact that the world is at her feet. This adoration used to terrify her, Now she quite enjoys the effect she has."

Neither Diana nor Charles had been happy in their marriage, but neither also had wanted to divorce. The Queen wanted it. Diana told the Queen she would only agree on a separation. Neither she nor Charles wanted to divorce. The Queen reluctantly agreed and on December 9, 1992, the royal couple issued a joint statement that after eleven years of marriage, they had agreed to a separation.

Diana hired several different women be nannies for her sons, for times when she was away on humanitarian or charitable work. She was jealous of the nannies' time with the boys and fired them. She was especially jealous of a nanny the boys called "Tiggy' (Alexandra Legge-Bourke) who cared for the boys from 1993 to 1999 (after Diana's death in 1997).

It has been said here and by other biographers that the royal couple's marital problems went back to before their marriage and continued throughout it. In 1985, four years into their marriage, Charles and Diana visited President Ronald Reagan and his wife Nancy in the White House. It was a pleasant break from the royal couple's marital troubles. Diana especially enjoyed dancing with Reagan, John Travolta, Neil Diamond, and Clint Eastwood. Charles danced with Nancy Reagan and they afterward became pen pals.

Diana Pearl wrote in *People* magazine in 2017 that in his letter to Nancy Reagan on June 21, 1992, six months before his separation from Diana, Prince Charles described his marriage to Princess Diana as "It's a kind of Greek tragedy, and would certainly make a very good play. It's so awful, very few people would believe it. No one can really understand what it all means until it happens to you, which is why it all keeps getting worse and worse."

Charles wrote Nancy Reagan that he had taken to reading classic literature as a distraction from the headlines about his marriage. He said he hoped it would make him "wiser and more knowledgeable."

He said, "One day I will tell you the whole story."

It is likely that Charles read some ancient Greek tragedies, because of his reference to them in his own life. Greek tragedies date from the 5th Century BC. They are stage plays in which, by definition, "a protagonist, usually a person of importance and outstanding personal qualities, falls to disaster through the combination of a personal failing and circumstances with which he or she cannot deal."

Nancy Reagan and Prince Charles had childhood traumas in common. Her parents divorced when she was just a few years old and her mother remarried when Nancy was eight.

Prince Charles may have been preaching to the choir when he wrote to Nancy Reagan about his mixed-up love life, loving another woman while married to Diana. Kitty Kelly wrote in her biography of Nancy that when Nancy Davis was a film starlet, she was sexually active in Hollywood, dating Clark Gable, Robert Stack, and Peter Lawford. She was single but may not have been a virgin when she married Reagan.

Nancy Reagan met and became attracted to singer-actor Frank Sinatra at a Reagan California gubernatorial campaign function in 1966. Sinatra, according to his later wife film actress Ava Gardner, was one of the most largely endowed men in Hollywood, which appealed to Mrs. Reagan.

Kelly said that while married to President Reagan, the First Lady invited Frank Sinatra to the White House often and instructed the staff "not to disturb them," even if the President asked for her. Sinatra would enter the White House through a back door to have private lunches with her. Nancy and Sinatra were rumored to have slept together and began an affair.

Meanwhile, biographer Darwin Porter wrote that President Reagan had been a womanizer who slept with more than 50 beautiful Hollywood actresses in a three-bedroom bungalow on the grounds of the Garden of Allah Hotel in Los Angeles in the 1940s and 1950s. The handsome All American Boy actor's bed mates included Marilyn Monroe, Lana Turner, and Doris Day, during and after he was married to film actress Jane Wyman from 1940 to 1949. During that marriage he also was in an affair with "Oomph Girl" film actress Ann Sheridan, his co-star in two films including his best, "Kings Row" in 1942.

Also before his marriage to Nancy, Reagan reportedly was in love with another young film actress, Catherine Lawson. Nothing is known of her career or life. Reagan is said to have continued seeing her during his marriage to Nancy. So goes the love lives of the rich and famous.

It's doubtful that Nancy Reagan admitted her extra-marital love life, including the infidelities, in her exchange of letters with Prince Charles. He may have been more revealing in his missiles to her.

Privately, Princess Diana explained to her son William, then 10 years old, about her separation from his father: "There were three of us in this marriage and the pressure of the media was another factor, so the two together were very difficult, that although I still loved Papa, I couldn't live under the same roof as him, and likewise with him." She said she "put it gently, without resentment or any anger."

Four television interviews then sealed the fate on the royal couple's marriage.

First, Charles, in an interview on June 29, 1994 with Jonathan Dimbleby on television admitted, "I was unfaithful to Diana. But I didn't hate her. It was only after the marriage had disintegrated beyond repair after about five years, possibly as late as 1986." He did not name Camilla Parker Bowles, merely said she was a longtime great friend. He said he was not intimate with the woman he loved until he believed his marriage was hopeless.

Millions watched the interview and were shocked; especially the Queen.

8

Charles's Television Interview

Prince Charles and Princess Diana had been separated for well over a a year when he gave a sensational interview on television on June 29, 1994. Neither wanted a divorce, so the Queen almost commanded them to separate.

Charles gave the interview to get back at Diana after her 1992 tell-all book was published. *Diana: Her True Story*, written by her biographer, Andrew Morton, the princess not only exposed Charles' love for Camilla. She let several cats out of the bag. She revealed that because of her husband's infidelity, she became unfaithful in return, with several men. [*At least eleven.*]

Prince Charles began the interview by trying to soften his image, telling about his philanthropy. He then went on about his role within the royal family, and his views on religion, architecture and the environment. Then he let a very big cat out of the bag.

Jonathan Dingleby asked Charles, "Had you been faithful and honorable during your marriage?"

Charles replied, "Yes, absolutely."

"And you were?" he was asked.

Charles said, "Yes. Until it [*his marriage*] became irretrievably broken down, us both having tried."

Charles did not admit that Camilla Parker Bowles was the woman with whom he had been unfaithful to Diana. He skirted around identifying her by name, just saying she was "a great friend" who had been "Important and helpful."

Stop the presses! Tabloids revealed news of the red-hot interview 48 hours before it ran on television.

Many of the millions who watched or read about the interview wondered why Charles answered the personal and sensitive questions and why he gave those answers.

Charles's deputy private secretary, Stephen Langport, said "There may have been some naivete as to how people would react, but I don't think that was the driving force. As strange as it sounds given the nature of the confession. I think it was basic honesty. Charles isn't a liar, and it's not in his nature to not consider and answer questions thoughtfully and, yes, honestly."

By far, most of the public judged that in the royal wedding the villain was the husband. Charles may have thought he needed to work a little on his public speaking. Diana celebrated by going to a dance wearing a revealing black gown. She looked beautiful, even radiant.

9

Margaret and Diana

Princess Margaret, the Countess of Snowdon, was the youngest daughter of King George VI and Queen Elizabeth II [*Mary, the Queen Mother*]. Margaret wanted to marry handsome British Air Force Group Captain Peter Townsend in 1953, but he was divorced and the Anglican Church did not sanction his remarriage. A year later she married photographer Anthony Armstrong-Jones, a notorious playboy, in 1960. They were often in tabloid news since they took separate vacations and had affairs with others. in between having two children together. They separated in 1976 and divorced two years later, making Margaret the first royal to divorce since Henry VIII ended his 24-year marriage to Catherine of Aragon in 1531.

When Princess Diana moved into Kensington Palace in 1981 before her marriage to Prince Charles, she thought she had a friend in Princess Margaret, Charles's niece and the Queen's younger sister. Margaret had been one of the first to welcome Diana to the House of Windsor, but later learned that "Her Rude Highness" had become her bitter enemy.

Margaret and Diana both had apartments at Kensington Palace and saw each other frequently. The Queen asked Margaret to take Diana under her wing and instruct her about her duties as a soon-to-be member of the royal family when she and Charles were married.

Margaret tutored Diana in how she was expected to conduct herself at social gatherings, even whose hand she was to shake. Margaret herself was a heavy smoker and drinker, but suggested that Diana abstain from both.

Their falling-out as friends was not only because Margaret was not only jealous of all the media attention Diana was getting. She became furious with her for exposing the royal family to scandal in Andrew Morton's 1992 book. It incensed her that Diana had virtually dictated the tell-all book to Morton. Queen Mary, who also disliked Diana, added to Diana's stress in her marriage.

Margaret was unforgiving of those who criticized the royal family. She stopped talking to Diana, would not let her children talk to her, and turned over magazines that pictured her. She bad-mouthed Diana to her friends and called her a "wretched girl."

Margaret did not hide her feelings about Diana's death. She was visibly uncaring.

When a campaign began to have a statue erected in front of Kensington Palace where Margaret lived, she said, "I'm not having that woman outside my bedroom window."

The statue was never built, but Diana's sons William and Harry keep the idea alive.

10

Diana's Panorama Interview

D iana lived with the public humiliation from her estranged husband's television interview for more than a year. She felt that the "men in blue," Charles's allies at Buckingham Palace, were plotting to get rid of her, or at least to marginalize her and possibly take her sons away from her, so she fought back. This took the retaliating form of admitting in her own television interview about her loveless marriage. The interview was full of British royal bombshells.

She kept it top secret, but in 1995 she was having herself interviewed on videotape by Martin Bashir, a Pakistani-British journalist, for a book she ached to have published. The sensational tapes were televised on the BBC program, *Panorama*, on November 20, 1995. She revealed a lot of scandalous things about herself, her husband, their unhappy and unfaithful marriage, the Queen, the British monarchy's future, and the tabloid media and paparazzi invasion of her privacy. Her revelations and concerns pulled no punches and took no prisoners as it shocked millions of viewers around the world.

Diana confessed that she had more than enough of Charles, Camilla, the Queen, and told how she had felt unwanted and unloved during her so-far 14-year marriage to the prince of her dreams. She said her friends agreed with her: her marriage had been at the start and still was a living nightmare.

Millions of her fans could hardly believe their ears. Their beloved "Princess of the People" was, to many Brits, like a perfect woman, a virgin yet a beautiful young "Earth Mother."

Within a few short hours, a London newspaper headlined the interviews that opened with a transcript of the tapes. Around the world, the headline word of the evening had been spoken, and by the Princess herself. The word was *unfaithful*.

The Diana tapes and her revelations in the interviews were far beyond what many expected to hear. Many gasped when she said another woman was stealing her husband. Unlike Charles had, Diana gave her rival a name, Camilla Parker Jones.

Diana's and Charles's separation was in its third year when the tapes were aired. The world heard Diana say her famous words about her marriage: "There were three of us in this marriage, so it was a little crowded."

Bashir asked how Diana knew about Charles's love for Camilla. She replied, "Oh, a woman's instinct is a very good one." She added that some Buckingham Palace staff had told her about the other woman for her husband's affections. "People who minded and cared for our marriage." She said that when she saw her rival with Charles, she could tell they loved each other.

Diana dropped another bombshell by revealing she had been in a romantic relationship with her riding instructor, James Hewitt, in 1986, while she had been married for five years but was getting no love from her unfaithful husband. She further shocked her public by telling of other men with whom she had had some romantic relations.

Bashir asked about her relationship with James Hewitt, her riding instructor during her marriage.

"I adored him!" Diana said. "Yes, I was in love with him." But she said she had turned to him only because she was getting no love from her unfaithful husband.

"But I was terribly let down [*by Hewitt*]." He was extensively quoted in a book that she strongly objected to. She felt that he had betrayed her trust, and he hoped to cash in on his romance with her. However, her fears on that score were unfounded, because he did not take financial advantage of their relationship.

Bashir asked, "Do you really believe that a [*palace*] campaign was being waged against you?"

Diana replied, "Yes, I did, absolutely; yeah."

Bashir asked, "Why?"

Diana said, "I was the separated wife of the Prince of Wales. I was a problem, full stop. 'Never happened before, what do we do with her?'"

Bashir asked if she would prefer that her son William succeed the Queen, and she said, "My wish is that my husband finds peace of mind, and from that follows other things."

Diana spoke on many subjects and near the end of the program, he asked her: "Looking back now do you feel at all responsible for the difficulties in your marriage?"

Diana said, "Mmm. I take full responsibility. I take some responsibility that our marriage went the way it did. I'll take half of it, but I won't take any more than that."

Bashir asked Diana why she had decided to give the highly controversial interview and play the tapes for her future book. She replied, "Because we will have been separated three years this December, and the [*tabloid media's*] perception that has been given of me for the last three years has been very confusing, turbulent, and in some areas I'm sure many, many people doubt me.

"And I want to reassure all those people who have loved me and supported me throughout the last 15 years that I will never let them down. That is a priority to me, along with my children."

Diana concluded, "I don't sit here with resentment. I sit here with sadness that a marriage hasn't worked. I sit here with hope because there's a future ahead, a future for my husband, a future for myself, and a future for the monarchy." She said the royal family was in desperate need of modernization and to become closer to the people.

She further shocked her public by telling of other men with whom she had had some romantic relations.

She had done the unthinkable. She had dared to criticize the Queen, and on worldwide television. Talk about her new increase in self-confidence.

When asked if she thought she ever would become Queen, she replied, "I'd like to be a Queen of people's hearts. But I don't see myself being

Queen of the country. I don't think many people will want me to be Queen."

Bashir asked what were the expectations she had for married life? Diana replied, "I think any marriage, especially when you've had divorced parents like myself, you'd want to try even harder to make it work and you don't want to fall back into a pattern that you've seen happen in your own family. I desperately wanted [*my marriage*] to work. I desperately loved my husband, and I wanted to share everything together. I thought we were a very good team."

She was asked how aware she was of the significance of what happened to her after her marriage because she might become Queen. Diana said, "I wasn't daunted, and am not daunted by the responsibilities that [*my*] role creates. It was a challenge. It is a challenge. As for becoming Queen, it's, it was never at the forefront of my mind when I married my husband. It was a long way off that thought."

Diana then said, "The most daunting aspect [*of her marriage*] was the media attention, because my husband and I, we were told when we got engaged that the media would go away quietly, and it didn't. And then when we were married, they said it would go away quietly, and it didn't. And then it started to focus very much on me, and I seemed to be on the front of a newspaper every single day, which is an isolating experience, and the higher the media put you, place you, is the bigger the drop. And I was very aware of that."

Bashir asked, "How did you handle the transition from being Lady Diana Spencer to the most photographed, the most talked-about woman in the world?"

Diana replied, "Well, it took a long time to understand why people were so interested in me, but I assumed it was because my husband had done a lot of wonderful work leading up to our marriage and our relationship. But then, during the years you see yourself as a good product that sits on a shelf and sells well, and people make a lot of money out of you... The media were everywhere. Here was a fairy tale story that everybody wanted to work."

Diana said she and Charles made a six-week tour of Australia and two-weeks in New Zealand early in their marriage. He encouraged her to walk across the street and talk to the people, as he did on his side. "I said 'I can't. I just can't.' He said, 'Well, you've got to do it.' And he went off and did his bit, and I did mine. It practically finished me off there and then. I went back to our hotel room and realized the impact that, you know, I had to sort myself out."

"When we flew back from New Zealand, I was a different person. I realized the sense of duty, the level of intensity of interest, and the demanding role I now found myself in."

Bashir asked if at that early stage, did she feel she was happily married? "Very much so," she answered. "But the pressure on us both as a couple with the media was phenomenal, and misunderstood by a great many people."

Then the green-eyed monster came between them. She said, "We'd be going round Australia, for instance, and all you could hear was, 'Oh, she's on the other side.' Now, if you're a man, like my husband a proud man, you mind if you hear it every day for four weeks"

Bashir asked, "So they were expressing a preference even then for you rather than your husband?"

"Yes," Diana said, "which I felt very uncomfortable with, and I felt it was unfair, because I wanted to share."

He asked if she had been flattered by the media attention? "No, because with the media attention came a lot of jealousy. A great deal of complicated situations arose because of that."

The humanitarian developed. "I found myself being more and more involved with people who were rejected by society... drug addicts, alcoholics, battered this, battered that...and I felt an affinity there... Then I found myself being more and more involved with people who were rejected by society - with, I'd say, drug addicts, alcoholism, battered this, battered that - and I found an affinity there.

"No one sat me down with a piece of paper and said: 'This us what is expected of you.' I'm lucky enough in the fact that I have found my role, and I'm very conscious of it, and I love being with people. I remember when I used to sit on hospital beds and hold people's hands, people used to be sort of shocked because they said they'd never seen this before, and to me it was quite a normal thing to do... And when I saw the reassurance that an action like that gave, I did it everywhere and will always do that."

She then told about her post-natal depression, after giving birth to William. The royal family thought I was mentally unbalanced. Unfortunately, that seems to have stuck on and off over the years."

Diana then discussed her bulimia eating disorder. "The cause was because my husband and I had to keep everything together... We didn't want to disappoint the public, and yet obviously there was a lot of anxiety going on within our four walls."

She said that she and Charles had separate hotel bedrooms when they traveled.

Bashir asked what effect the media interest in her have on her marriage. "It made it very difficult," she said, "because for a situation where it was a couple working in the same job. We got out the same car, my husband did the speeches, I did the handshaking, so basically we were a married couple doing the same job, which is very difficult for anyone, and more so if you've got all the attention on you.

"We struggled a bit with it, it was very difficult, and then my husband decided that we do separate engagements, which was a bit sad for me, because I quite liked the company."

On the very personal side, Diana said that to Charles and the rest of the royal family, "I think I've always been the 18-year-old girl he got engaged to, so I don't think I've been given any credit for growth. And, my goodness, I've had to grow.

"Anything good I ever did nobody ever said a thing, never said, 'Well done!' But if I tripped up, which invariably I did... a ton of bricks came down on me."

Diana said she felt isolated in her marriage. "There's no better way to dismantle a personality than to isolate it."

Bashir asked about her separation from Charles. She said, "My husband asked for the separation and I supported it... I felt deep, deep, profound sadness. Because we had struggled to keep it going, but obviously we'd both run out of steam. And in a way, I suppose it could have been a relief for us both... It was not my idea. Not at all. I come from a divorced background, and I didn't want to go into that one again... The fairy tale had come to an end."

She said she actually learned about it [*the separation*] on the radio. William gave her a box of chocolates, to try to cheer her up.

Diana said the royal family was now a problem, still rejecting her because she was independent. "But I won't go quietly... I'll fight to the end, because I believe that I have a role to fulfill, and I've got two children to bring up."

Bashir asked, "Looking back now, do you feel at all responsible for the difficulties in your marriage?"

Diana replied, "Mmm. I take full responsibility, I take some responsibility that our marriage went the way it did. I'll take half of it, but I won't take any more than that, because it takes two to get in this situation... We both made mistakes."

She was asked what role she saw for herself in the future. She said, "I would like to be an ambassador for this country. I'd like to represent this country abroad, and its good qualities."

When asked about what changes she would like to see in the monarchy, she said, "I think they could walk hand-in-hand [*with the people*], as opposed to be so distant...I don't mean by riding round bicycles... but just having a more in-depth understanding."

Bashir asked about a possible divorce. Diana replied, "I don't want a divorce... I await my husband's decision of which way we are all going to go... It's not my wish... What about the children? Our boys. That's what matters, isn't it? My wish is that my husband finds peace of mind.

"I don't sit here with resentment. I sit here with sadness because a marriage hasn't worked. I sit here with hope because there's a future ahead, a future for my husband, a future for myself, and a future for the monarchy."

Diana later said she regretted giving the very candid interview. She had hoped it would help her, but it didn't. It only made things worse for her with the royal family.

11

Charles's Other Mistress

Diana's other biographers do not mention it, but she had another serious rival besides Camilla Parker Bowles for Prince Charles's affections during her engagement to him and even in her marriage to him. She was Lady Dale Tryon, a beautiful, vivacious Australian-born blonde fashion designer whom Charles nicknamed "Kanga," short for kangaroo, after which she named her line of designer dresses.

It is known that she pursued Charles after he married, and fantasized of being his Queen. Charles said that Dale "was the only woman who understood me."

Dale was born Dale Elizabeth Harper in Melbourne, Australia on January 3, 1948, the daughter of a wealthy publisher. After college, she moved to London in 1972 where she became popular in society. A few months after her arrival, while she worked in public relations for an airline, she met young Baron Anthony Tryon, an aristocrat who was a member of Prince Charles's inner circle.

Tryon introduced Dale to Prince Charles at a ball later in 1972, and the beautiful belle of the balls and parties and the world's most eligible bachelor and potential future King of England were instantly attracted to each other. They discovered that both enjoyed fly fishing and soon began going on fishing outings in Iceland, joined by her husband. He seemed to tolerate her attraction to the Prince, or could do nothing about it because Charles was of such high royalty. That was pretty stiff competition.

Dale's friendship with Charles developed into a romantic relationship while he was in search of a wife. It was widely accepted in British society that if a man was to have a mistress, she was to be a married woman, because if the affair was exposed, she would have more to lose than he.

Dale Tryon and Camilla Parker Bowles knew that Charles was having an affair with both of them and became bitter jealous rivals. Diana had known about Charles's love for Camilla before her engagement to the prince. During their engagement, she learned of Charles' affair with Dale. Both affairs troubled her, but Diana worried more about Camilla's hold on the prince. In 1974, Dale became Charles's favorite mistress, for a while.

Dale had opened a fashion shop and Diana began buying her dresses and gowns. Despite knowing that Charles and Dale were in an affair together, Diana and Dale became sort-of friends in the 1980s. Diana wore Kanga dresses to intentionally snub Camilla.

Dale married Lord Anthony Tryon in 1973 and they remained married until his death in 1997. Camilla married British Army Brigadier Andrew Parker Bowles in 1973 and they divorced in 1995. Diana and Charles married in 1981, separated in 1992, and divorced in 1996. Camilla and her first husband had two children together, while Dale and her husband had four. Charles became godfather for each of their sons.

Dale was heartsick when Diana and Charles separated in 1992 because she feared that he would turn to Camilla, which he did. It especially distressed Dale when Charles threw a lavish 50th birthday party for Camilla at Highgrove on July 17, 1997.

Dale began suffering from cancer and mental illness. While in hospital in early 1997, she fell out of a window. Rumors were that she did not fall but had jumped out of a first floor window, in despair over Charles's love for Camilla and that her rival would become Queen of England. She broke her back and became paralyzed. Her husband then asked for a divorce.

Dale denied that she had attempted suicide, but her life was falling apart. She became a paranoid paraplegic in a wheelchair until her death in London on November 15, 1997. It was just four months after Diana died on August 31.

Ironically, Dale had been living at the Ritz Hotel in Paris when Diana had been living there with Dodi Fayed. It is not known if Dale learned of Diana's death in the car crash.

She never knew that her rival eventually won the man she fatally loved. Charles and Camilla were married in a civil ceremony on April 9, 2005.

12

The Divorce

After Diana's *Panorama* television interview in 1995, the Queen wrote to both Diana and Charles. She asked them to seek an early divorce for the good of the empire. They agreed and the divorce was finalized on August 28, 1996.

Under terms of the divorce, Diana lost her title as Her royal Highness and was thereafter known as Princess of Wales. She was allowed to continue living in Buckingham Palace and to keep all her jewelry, plus she was awarded an alimony settlement of the British equivalent of $26 million as well as a generous monthly allowance. She would be involved in all decisions about her sons and would share custody of them with Charles.

While it may seem that Charles was largely to blame for the divorce, some such as Sally Bedell Smith lays some of it on Diana. In her book *Diana in Search of Herself,* she wrote: "During Diana's lifetime, few were willing to confront directly the extent of her emotional problems. For the first half of her life, when she was usually in a protected environment, Diana managed to keep her problems in check, except for occasional flare-ups when she was in stressful situations. Just turned twenty [when she married Charles], Diana was often out of control, her fragile psyche cracking under the strain of public life."

Dr. Michael Adler, chairman of the National AIDS Trust, agreed. He knew Diana from her visits to AIDS patients, and said "She clearly should have had a lot more professional help. I think she needed rather intense professional counseling and psychological support, and I was never certain that she ever had that in a manner that I would have thought was totally helpful."

Smith said, "Prince Charles, who witnessed her extreme behavior longer than anyone, lacked the knowledge and temperament to help her deal with her torment. He probably deserves more credit than he has received for trying to get her into therapy on several occasions.

"It may ultimately be impossible to fully explain Diana because she was so mercurial. Even those close to her had trouble grasping what was going on in her mind."

What was going on in Diana's mind at her wedding was, she reportedly told her sisters, "It was the worst day of my life." She said she was not sure if she could go through with the wedding. "I can't marry him. I can't do this. This is absolutely unbelievable."

What troubled Diana on the eve of her marriage was mainly that her husband-about-to-be loved Camilla Parker Bowles and not her.

Her sisters encouraged her to "push through" with the marriage because tea towels and other memorabilia of the event with her face on it already had been printed and purchased by royal family followers all over the world. Diana wanted to please, so she took a deep breath and went through with the wedding.

Charles felt that his father Prince Philip had bullied him into marrying Diana, according to Sally Bedell Smith. Philip wrote Charles a letter that he thought Charles was tarnishing Diana's reputation by not marrying her. He said, "propose or break up."

Prince Philip reportedly was not always faithful to Queen Elizabeth during their so-far 70-year marriage. Author Gyles Brandreth claimed that Philip had been romantically involved with an unnamed woman whom he met on a regular basis in the West End apartment of a society photographer.

While Elizabeth wore the crown, Philip was reportedly the one who was the power behind the throne. He was said to be shrewd, steadfast, and always supportive.

Bedell wrote that she did not see Charles as being a cynical person in marrying Diana without loving her. He thought he could learn to love her, as his grandmother Queen Mother Mary and grandfather King George V learned to love each other and have a successful marriage.

But, Bedell wrote, the Diana-Charles marriage was doomed before it began, because of their age differences, interest incompatibilities, his love for Camilla, and Diana's emotional turmoil.

Diana continued to visit sick children and elderly, but went on to champion humanitarian causes, over time becoming patron or president of 100 of them including those representing HIV, AIDS, leprosy, spinal injury research, wildlife preservation, the deaf, head injuries, the aged. Charles also was patron of many causes but mainly those involving the arts.

Because of Diana's philanthropic activism it became harder than ever for Charles's regal ego to cope with the attention the media showered on her. He was not used to being in anyone's shadow, especially playing second fiddle to his wife. He was the future King of England. If Diana, a former kindergarten teacher's aid, was now called "The People's Princess," who had he become, a plate of chopped liver? It was the old Hollywood story of the supporting actor stealing the picture from the star.

Charles said, jokingly to an audience of men at a formal reception which she did not attend, "I have come to the conclusion that I should have had two wives, to cover both sides of the streets [*during his and Diana's public appearances*]. And I could have walked down the middle directing the operation."

There was another reason Charles had grown unhappy with Diana. A year before their divorce, he believed she and her best friend, his sister-in-law Sarah Ferguson, were telling others they doubted he was suitable to be King. He began to believe that they were sabotaging him so Fergie's husband, his brother Prince Andrew, could become King instead. As of 2019, Andrew is actually 8th in line for the crown.

13

The Humanitarian

After her divorce, Diana's picture made front pages everywhere as she was photographed not afraid to touch or even hug AIDS patients. She began to realize how important touching them and others was. She learned touching and other bedside manner skills from a hospital nurse, Muriel Stevens.

Said Stevens, "The first thing I taught Diana was to stoop down so she was always on the patient's eye level. It was important as many were in wheelchairs. The second was to always get hold of their hands. An instant physical contact. It also meant for a young person like Di who was very pretty, [*elderly*] patients would want to touch her face."

Diana often took her sons with her to visit the sick and dying, even to AIDS patients. She said, "I wanted them to have an understanding of people's emotions, people's insecurities, of people's hopes and dreams."

Diana at other times said "The worst illness of our time is that so many people have to suffer from never being loved." And " Two things stand like stone... kindness in another's troubles and courage in your own."

Diana's friends began to notice a change in her as she noticeably gained self-confidence from her volunteer work.

"Diana is on a voyage of discovery," said one of her close friends. "What we are seeing is her real personality coming through. She will make mistakes, but ultimately we will see a genuine manifestation of the real person."

A nurse in a children's hospital said, "Doing humanitarian work, Diana has got in touch with her own nature and has found a new confidence and sense of liberation which she had never known before."

Angela Serota, a dancer with the royal Ballet, said that as a result of Diana's social work, "I thought she was utterly beautiful in a very profound way. She has an inner spirit which shines forth though there was also a sense of pervasive unhappiness about her."

While Diana showed an increase in self-confidence, by 1990 she also showed strains of nine years in a marriage in which she felt unloved and in a world spotlight she no longer could tolerate.

Shortly before her divorce in 1996, Diana confirmed what humanitarian work meant to her by saying, "People [women] think that at the end of the day, a man is the answer. Actually, a fulfilling job is better for me."

In January of 1997, just a few months before the tragic car crash that would take her life, Princess Diana stepped out onto an active minefield in Angola in south-central Africa to watch mine workers clear away explosives. Landmines were left hidden during Angola's war for independence from Portugal between 1961 and 1974. They were still causing casualties and taking lives indiscriminately.

Never one to shy away from a difficult cause, Diana knew full well the publicity a trip like this would generate for the then-controversial issue, and she was right. Advocating against landmines became her last humanitarian cause.

Diana did not personally win the Nobel Peace Prize for her anti-personal landmine activism, but the Campaign to Ban Landmines, which she promoted, was awarded the prize a few months after her death in 1997.

PART TWO

The Men in Diana's Life

Besides her father and husband, there were at least eleven other men who were in Princess Diana's romantic life. Diana believed in astrology. Traditionally, thirteen is an unlucky number. The eleven were either her lovers or men with whom Diana was in some degree of a relationship, either known or rumored by others who knew her well.

Diana's lovers were a lot alike, her bodyguard Ken Wharfe wrote in his 2002 book *Diana: Closely Guarded Secret*. "Lined up in an identity parade, then one would hardly be able to tell them apart. All were tall, of similar physique [*well-built*], dressed and spoke in the same manner, shared the same tastes and the same circle of friends, and often the same mannerisms. "They may have differed slightly, but all had one thing in common: they were nothing like her serious-minded husband."

We learn more about Diana from learning more about these men who entered her life, in chronological order.

1

John Spencer, the 8th Earl Spencer

Diana's father, known as Lord Spencer or Viscount Althorp, was the only son and younger child of Albert Spencer, 7th Earl of Spencer. Known to his family as Johnnie Althorp, he was educated at Eaton College and the Royal Military College.

He served as Captain in the royal Scots Greys from 1944 to 1945. From 1947 to 1950, he served as aide-de-camp to his Excellency Lieutenant-General Sir Willoughby Norriem then governor of South Australia.

He later served as equerry (*military aid*) to King George VI and Queen Mary and was invested as a member of the royal Victorian Order in 1954. He became the 8th Earl Spencer upon the death of his father in 1975, when Diana was fourteen years old.

Diana was his third daughter. He had wanted a son instead, to make up for the son his wife Frances had given him earlier but who died after a few days. Frances Spencer loved another man and left home when Diana was six. Her parents divorced two years later and both entered other marriages. She did not like her stepmother and was reared by nannies she also did not like.

Lord Spencer served in the House of Lords from 1975 when he inherited the peerage to his death in 1992 at the age of 68.

Diana grew up knowing that her father did not want her at her birth and thereafter she felt unloved by him.

2

Charles, Prince of Wales

Diana's husband was rarely if ever sympathetic to her about the load she carried for him, the Queen, and her country. One day early in their marriage, his love Camilla Parker Bowles telephoned at Buckingham Palace and had a complaint for him.

He listened, then hung up and agonized to Diana, "Poor Camilla Parker Bowles. She said there are a lot of newsmen around her house tonight [*and she is upset*]." Diana asked, "How many press are out there?" He replied, "She said, 'At least four.'"

Diana thought, but never told him, "My God, there are *thirty-four* here!"

Diana's husband was born Charles Philip Arthur George on November 14, 1948 in Buckingham Palace, the eldest son of Queen Elizabeth II and Prince Philip, the Duke of Edinburgh and her consort. Like Diana, he had a lonely and mostly unhappy childhood.

The Queen was delighted with her first-born and breast-fed him his first two months, but then had to stop because she contracted measles. His mother usually saw him only twice a day, in the morning and just before bedtime, for a half-hour each time.

She was often away from him during his infancy, attending to royal duties and spending as much time as she could with her husband. She was reportedly not indifferent [*to infant Charles*] so much as detached. Charles found some comfort in his dog, a corgi who was called Sugar.

Philip was an officer in the royal Navy and away a lot, so young Charles did not see him much. A year after Charles was born, his father was posted to Malta.

Philip saw little of Charles for the first two years of his son's life. When he was home in the palace, Philip taught young Charles to shoot, fish, and swim in the palace pool. On a fatherly level, however, Philip was alternately distant or combative. Charles later called him "harsh" and "hectoring."

As a boy, Charles was "easily cowered by the forceful personality of his father," Jonathan Dimbleby wrote in his biography of Charles. "Philip was brusque with his young son, belittling and even bullying him." This often brought the little boy to tears.

Philip admitted that he and his son were as different as they could be. "Charles is a romantic, and I am a pragmatist," he told biographer Gyles Brandreth in 2016. "That means we do things differently. And because I don't see things as a romantic would, [*he thinks*] I'm unfeeling."

Philip had similar problems with his own father, whom he hardly knew and rarely saw as a boy. Both Charles and Philip grew up without father figures from whom to receive affection.

Charles was sensitive from the start, said Sally Bedell Smith in her biography of Charles. She said his finely-tuned antennae were susceptible to slights and rebukes. His father noticed this and worried that his son would become weak and vulnerable, so he began to toughen him up.

Charles and his father were actually opposites in personality.

Neither the Queen nor Philip showed Charles or his sister Anne much parental affection. Upon returning to the palace in 1954 after an almost six-month tour of Commonwealth nations, the parents gave their five-year-old son and three-year-old daughter a handshake instead of a hug and kiss.

Charles got more affection from his grandmother. As a boy, when his parents were away, he visited Queen Mother Mary often at royal Lodge, her home in Windsor Great Park. She gave him the hugs he craved but didn't get from his parents. As early as two, he would sit on her bed and play with her lipsticks. She introduced him to the worlds of art and classical music. He didn't think his parents appreciated either.

"My grandmother was the person who taught me to look at things," he said. She encouraged his kind and gentle nature, his eagerness to share his candy with other children. When choosing sides for games, he was to select the weakest first for his team. At the same time, his grandmother' protective side allowed him to engage in self-pity and his habit of "whinging," the British word for "whining." That infuriated his father.

Charles' parents wanted him to have a normal childhood without princely benefits. He went to a private school in London, but took a bus to get there, and was made to sweep the classroom floors. After only six months there, shortly before his ninth birthday, his father had him transferred to the boarding school he had attended, Cheam School, in Hampshire. He was homesick there and often, in private, clutched his teddy bear and cried.

He was bullied at school where the other boys made fun of his protruding ears. They also called him "Prince Pudgy" because he was slightly overweight. Like Diana later, he ate snacks to relax.

He knew he was a loner. "I've often preferred my own company, or just a one to one," Charles said later.

He was sick sometimes, from sinus infections and had a tonsillectomy. He was hospitalized with Asian flu, but his parents didn't visit him. They were on tour in India when he came down with measles at age 12. Charles was no good at rugby, cricket, soccer or other sports in school, being physically uncoordinated as well as overweight. He also was not comfortable on horseback. Polo was out for him.

His father, an avid horseman and polo player, thought that was unmanly.

Academically, Charles was good at art and music but bad at mathematics. His mother considered him to be "a slow developer."

What Charles enjoyed at Cheam was appearing in school plays. He felt comfortable on stage.

Charles made no lasting friendship from his five years at Cheam. His grandmother The Queen Mother urged that his next school be Eton, in London, but his father thought his son unsuited for a "rough-and-tumble" school. Charles was enrolled at Gordonstoun, Philip's alma mater, in isolated northern Scotland. While most of her friends' sons went to Eaton, the Queen sided with Philip in choosing that distant college prep school.

Charles was miserable at Gordonstoun where he was again taunted because of his jug ears. The other boys were rough on him in rugby matches, but Charles was stoic and never fought back. The only boy with whom he became friends was Donald Greene, his bodyguard who was a few years older. The friendship began a pattern in which Charles preferred the company of his elders.

Philip was not satisfied with his son's progress toward manhood at Gordonstoun. When Charles was 17 years old in 1966, his father sent him to Australia where he spent two terms in the outback at Timbertop, the wilderness branch of the Geelong Church of England Grammar School in Melbourne.

Philip assigned his aide David Checketts to supervise Charles in Australia. Checketts had served in the royal Air Force, was 36 years old, of the middle class and down-to-earth. Charles liked him.

He also liked his new school, partly because none of the other boys taunted or bullied him. They didn't treat him like a prince but just one of the boys.

"There is no such thing as aristocracy or anything like it," Charles said of Australia." For the first time in his life, he was judged on "how people see you, and feel about you." Students and teachers treated him as one of them. To his surprise, he felt little homesickness.

He also liked it that the emphasis was not on academics but about physical challenges. He was surprised how he enjoyed them, finding he was up to cross-country expeditions in blistering heat, hiking 70 miles in three days and climbing three peaks along the way, and freezing nights outdoors in a sleeping bag. He also endures snakes, spiders, and endless flys and mosquitoes.

"It was jolly good for the character," Charles said, "and, in many ways, I loved it and learnt a lot from it."

Writing home about his rugged adventures, he hoped to prove to his father that he was not a weakling. His six months in Australia also brought him out of himself so that he felt at ease talking to others of any age.

Charles returned to Gordonstoun in the autumn of 1966 for his final year. He felt a new self-confidence from living down under and, his final year at Gordonstoun had now taught him self-control and self-discipline.

Charles then earned a Bachelor of Arts degree from the University of Cambridge. He then served in the royal Air Force and the royal Navy from 1971 to 1976.

His parents thought he was now ready to marry and have an heir. So did his favorite uncle, his father's brother Lord Earl Mountbatten.

"In a case like yours, " said Mountbatten, "the man should sew his wild oats and have as many affairs as he can before settling down."

Charles followed his uncle's advice. His girlfriends included Georgiana Russell, daughter of the British ambassador to Spain; Lady Jane Wellesley, daughter of the 8th Duke of Wellington; Davina Sheffield; and Camilla Shand who married to become Camilla Parker Bowles. In 1974, Mountbatten suggested a potential marriage to his granddaughter, Amanda Knatchbull, but her mother objected because Amanda was then only 16.

Charles, still in search of a wife, met Diana Spencer three years later at her home, Althorp, during a pheasant party. The rest is history.

3

Prince Philip

Princess Diana's relationship with her father-in-law Prince Philip, husband of Queen Elizabeth II, started out amicably when she married his son Prince Charles in 1981. It began to go downhill when she and Charles separated in 1992 and divorced in 1996, and she exposed royal family sexual indiscretions in her *Panorama* television interview in 1995. By the time of her death in 1997, she despised Philip, and the feeling was mutual.

Philip was born into Greek and Danish royal families on June 10, 1921, the son of Prince Albert of Greece+. He was born in Mon Repos on the Greek island of Corfu. His family was exiled from the country when he was an infant, after Greece lost its war with Turkey in 1922.

His mother, Alice of Battenberg, Germany, was deaf and was committed to a mental asylum in 1930 when he was nine. She remained institutionalized the rest of her life. His father had earlier left the family to live with a mistress, leaving Philip and his four sisters to live in orphanages. Philip visited his mother in mental hospitals over the years, but never saw his absent father. His mother had been well enough to attend his wedding. She died in 1969 at age 84. His father died in 1944 at age 64. Philip had not seen him since 1939 when Philip was 18.

Philip's boyhood and teen years were without normal parental closeness, much less love. His uncle Lord Earl Mountbatten became his surrogate father from when Philip was nine until he was 16. Philip was devastated by his uncle's assassination by Irish terrorists who blew up his yacht on August 27, 1979 at age 79. When Philip married the Queen on November 20, 1947, he could see his favorite uncle's coffin in Westminster Abbey.

Philip was educated in France, Germany, and the United Kingdom. While serving in the British Royal Navy when he was 18 in 1939, he and Princess Elizabeth, who was then 13, began corresponding. They had first met five years before. They became engaged in 1947 and Philip abandoned his Greek and Danish royal titles to become a naturalized British citizen, adopting his maternal grandparents' surname, Mountbatten. He left active Naval duty when Elizabeth became Queen in July 1947 and they married on November 20, 1947.

Philip has been credited with supporting the Queen over their 70-year marriage with utter devotion. One diplomat has said, "I've no doubt he has had a very wholesome effect on her. He helped to make her what she's become, She is very shrewd but had a protective shell around her, and he brought her out of it. We are extremely fortunate that he married her."

4

Barry Mannakee

B arry Mannakee and Princess Diana began a love affair in 1985 when he was assigned as her bodyguard. Their relationship began several months before Prince Charles renewed his affair with Camilla Parker Bowles, but at a time when Diana felt unloved by her husband.

Diana said in her secret videotapes, "In 1985, when I was 24 or 25, I fell deeply in love with someone who worked in the environment [*of her marriage*], and he was the greatest friend I ever had." She did not name him, but he was Barry Mannakee.

A police officer with the royal Protection Squad, Mannakee and Diana soon grew close, although he was married and the father of two children.

She said she saw him as a father figure. "I'm sure I did. I was like a little girl in front of him all the time. It was all found out and he was chucked out."

Sergeant Mannakee became Diana's confidant and something more. Rumors about their relationship circulated and it was considered "inappropriate." After a year protecting Diana, Mannakee was reassigned to the Diplomatic Protection Guard in London.

Diana said in her videotaped interview, "I should never have played with fire. And I did. I got very burned."

Inspector Ken Wharfe, Diana's later protector, wrote in his 2002 book *Diana: Closely Guarded Secret*, "He was summarily discharged [*from being Diana's bodyguard*] for overstepping the invisible mark of propriety between himself and Diana. Nothing was ever proved, but the rumor was strong enough, allegedly, for the Palace, fearing another royal scandal, instruct Scotland Yard to act to prevent a recurrence, The Queen had been aware of the relationship between her daughter, Princess Anne, and her protection officer, Sergeant Peter Cross, and he too had been moved from his job. The last thing the Palace wanted was for another serious transgression of this nature to become public."

Mannakee died in a motor crash in 1987, a year after he had stopped being Diana's bodyguard. He had been the passenger on a motorbike driven by fellow officer Steven Peat. In Woodford, northeast London, he crashed into a car driven by 17-year-old Nicola Chopp who had just passed her driving test six weeks earlier. Chopp had been waiting for a car to turn left, then pulled out, turning right across the motorbike's path. Peat swerved to avoid the car, but a collision occurred. Mannakee was thrown into the rear side window of Chopp's car and died instantly. Peat and Chopp both survived the crash.

An inquest concluded it had been an accident. However, both Diana and Chopp thought otherwise. Diana said Mannakee had been "bumped off" by British government security services because of their relationship.

Chopp said she had been pressured into admitting she was responsible for the collision. She described seeing "dazzling lights" from a "mystery car" at the time of the crash. "I have always wondered if some more sinister forces were at work that night, although I could never prove it. I believe, with conviction, I was not the cause of Barry Mannakee's death." However, no other vehicles were found to have been involved.

James Hewitt, another of Diana's levers, claimed years after Mannakee's death that he had been killed by rogue British Intelligence officers. "Without a shred of credible evidence, he suggested that they had somehow arranged a fatal accident [that took Mannakee's life.] Hewitt alleged that secret agents acting for the British Intelligence agencies planned to dispose of him just as they had Mannakee.

"He also claimed that Diana had told him that she and Mannakee had enjoyed a passionate affair. As 'proof,' he said that [*Mannakee*] had given Diana a brown teddy bear which she kept on her bed. According to Hewitt, when he saw it and observed that he thought it a rather intimate present for a policeman to give her, she said nonplussed, 'But we were lovers.'"

Wrote Wharfe, "It is undoubtedly true that Diana and Mannakee were very close, perhaps, in the eyes of the Palace and of Scotland Yard, too close. Because of the long hours spent in each other's company it was almost inevitable that a close friendship would grow between them. Having myself been the Princess' protection officer, I too became close to her, that it was the nature of the job."

Wharfe wrote that rumors that Diana and Mannakee were having an affair grew stronger in 1985. Senior members of Buckingham Palace staff complained to Prince Charles that Mannakee was showing signs of over-familiarity with Diana during public engagements. "Moreover," Wharfe wrote, "Diana, a natural flirt, was said to have encouraged [Mannakee] in his attentions.

"Finally, an unsubstantiated rumor began to circulate alleging that the two of them had been discovered in a compromising position by a senior member of Charles's staff on the eve of the wedding of the Duke and Duchess of York in July 1986. This proved to be the last straw. Just days after the alleged incident, Mannakee was moved to other duties in the Diplomatic Protection branch and out of Diana's life for good. A year later, he was dead."

Wharfe wrote, "Diana claimed that the allegations [involving her and Mannakee] were part of a smear campaign against her by Prince Charles's camp. Diana was not averse to embellishing the truth, but I believed her then and I still do [*in 2002*]. Undoubtedly, Mannakee, who was much older than her, became more than a policeman to her. He became a very close friend, a good listener whom she saw as a father figure, someone who would support her when she was down, and say "'You can cope, Diana.' Having been in much the same position myself, this has always struck me as the most convincing answer to the rumors [*of Diana's and Mannakee's relationship*]."

Wharfe wrote in his book on Diana, "When, in 1987, Prince Charles broke the news of Mannakee's accidental death as they were traveling to RAF Northolt where they would fly to Cannes for an official visit to the film festival, she burst into tears. But would she not? It was, after all, a natural reaction, especially in such an emotional woman who had just learned of the death of a close friend [*Mannakee*]. To suggest, however, that she went beyond simply crying on Mannakee's shoulder and began an affair with him is at best speculation of a particularly cruel kind, not in the least because both parties are dead and cannot therefore defend themselves.

"To suggest, however, as Hewitt did, that Mannakee was murdered because of their intimacy is the stuff of romantic thrillers.

After Mannakee's prophetic death in an automobile crash, she said, "I was only happy when he was around. It [*his death*] was the biggest blow of my life."

5

Bryan Adams

Princess Diana led a secret-filled life which extended to her numerous romantic relationships. She may have had a romantic affair with Canadian rock and roll singer Bryan Adams.

His girlfriend Cecile Thomsen said his affair with Diana was the reason she left him. "Ours was a stormy relationship, and Bryan's affair with Diana didn't make it easier. I know he had an affair with her," said Thomsen, a film actress who was a James Bond Girl.

Adams, however, denied he had been romantically linked to Diana, saying they were just "good friends." "Miss Thomsen doesn't know anything about my friendship with Diana, nor does anyone else. Anything you have read from these reporters is pure conjecture and supposition."

Adams was linked to Diana through a song he had written in 1985 early in his career before he met her. It was called "Diana," and in the lyrics, a man professes his love for a girl who married a man who is not good enough for her. He calls the girl the "Queen of my dreams." Adams sang his song at concerts for many years, but retired it after her death in 1997.

Thomsen accompanied Adams to Diana's funeral. She said, "I was sitting in the church with mixed emotion."

6

David Waterhouse

David Waterhouse was a big man with a big smile. He was a major in the Household Cavalry at Buckingham Palace in 1987 when he and Diana began an affair together.

A happy-go-lucky fellow, Diana enjoyed his quick wit and repartee. He livened parties she attended with her dour husband Prince Charles.

Waterhouse accompanied Diana and Charles on a ski holiday at Klosters in Switzerland in the winter of 1987. Five years later she nearly invited him on another holiday to Austria without Charles, but decided against it fearing the media attention it could create.

Waterhouse also escorted Diana to a David Bowie concert in London in 1987. Charles had not been interested in taking her because he detested rock and roll. She wore tight-fitting leather trousers to the concert, which shocked those at the palace when they saw photographs in the newspapers.

Diana was reportedly taken with Waterhouse at various times over the late 1980s and early 1990s. She turned to him for solace during her troubled years with Charles.

7

James Gilbey

James Gilbey was a close childhood friend of Diana's who later became an actor in the BBC television series *EastEnders* and then a television creative director for Discovery Networks Europe. Although neither of them admitted to having had a romantic relationship, they often saw each other during her marriage. He had a fun-loving nature and put Diana at ease during parties.

Gilbey's pet name for Diana was "Squidgy." He called her that 14 times and "darling" 53 times in phone calls in 1989. Ken Wharfe, another of Diana's bodyguards, wrote in his book about her that during Gilbey;'s calls to her, he told her he was looking forward to putting his 'warm, protective arms around [*her*] in a couple of days."

He became an innate part of Diana's life, even when she was seeing James Hewitt up to three times a week, according to Ken Wharfe in his 2002 book *Diana: Closely Guarded Secret*.

Gilbey was always around, completely obsessed with her, although she was never as close to him as she was to Hewitt. She found Gilbey to be an enjoyable distraction, not least for his urbanity.

Wharfe wrote that "although Gilbey was by no means her only or most significant admirer, the Princess, so long starved of love, found that she enjoyed beguiling more than one man at a time.

"As she grew in confidence, partly as a result of her affair with Hewitt, and partly because of the decisions she had taken about her life and work,

Diana was not afraid to play one admirer against another, so that there were times when she was enjoying the attentions of more than one man at a time."

Diana later played one admirer against another in her romance with Hasnat Khan, being intentionally photographed with Dodi Fayed so as to make Khan jealous when he refused to marry her, as we learn later.

"In order to do this [*have affairs with several men at the same time*], she increasingly came to rely on trusted friends to provide 'safe houses.' They were places where she could spend hours with a male admirer, confident of absolute privacy away from the prying eyes of servants, though with her faithful protection officer somewhere close at hand."Wharfe also said Diana's friends included mystics and fortune-tellers. She would spend hours locked away with these people whom she grew to depend on.

He said he regarded them with suspicious cynicism and told her so. She replied that although she doubted their veracity, she found them to be of increasing importance in her life. Each one told her a different story, and she seems perfectly happy to accept that, something that heightened her increasing insecurity, as well as the desperation of her quest to find solutions... any solutions... to the problems in her life."

The phone calls Gilbey made to Diana became known by the media as "Squidgygate." That was a humorous reference to Watergate, the United States' political scandal that forced President Richard Nixon to resign, although Diana and Gilbey had nothing to do with that.

Gilbey was one of the few friends who were loyal to Diana over her whole life. Diana said of Gilbey, "You were the rock that this wave of human emotion needed."

In 1992, while Diana's marriage to Prince Charles was imploding, a tape recording of a 30-minute telephone conversation between her and Gilbey was mysteriously obtained and made public. In the conversation, Gilbey told Diana he loved her. Despite Diana's non-committal replies of "you're so nice," the tape became one of the many scandals that hastened the end of her troubled marriage. One newspaper set up a 900 number where people could call in and listen to the tape for a fee.

Similarly, phone calls between Prince Charles and Camilla Parker Bowles had been taped, but later leaked. They were reportedly "insanely scandalous" and dubbed "Tampon gate." In one of their phone conversations, Charles told Camilla he would like to live in her underpants, perhaps as a tampon."

8

James Hewitt

James Hewitt, born in Derry, Northern Ireland, was in a five-year romantic relationship with Princess Diana that began in 1986. He had become an officer in the British Cavalry.

Hewitt and Diana met at a cocktail party given by her lady-in-waiting, Hazel West, in 1986. Diana liked how natural their first conversation was. He said he was a riding instructor. Diana said she was fearful when riding, and he offered to help her overcome that.

Soon after Hewitt became Diana's riding instructor, they became lovers. It came at a time when her marriage to Prince Charles was in trouble, strained by his love for Camilla Parker Bowles. Hewitt's and Diana's subsequent association was widely reported in the media.

Ken Wharfe wrote in his 2002 book *Diana: Closely Guarded Secret*, that "The Princess turned to Hewitt for solace and support, and I have little doubt that without him she would have been unable to cope."

Wharfe found Hewitt to be "a charming and very likable man.

For her part, Diana thought that she had at last found a man whom she could trust. He injected excitement and youthful vitality into her life at a time when she really needed to be loved." Charles sensed Diana was having an affair with Hewitt and welcomed it because he was having one with Camilla Parker Bowles. Charles and Diana were in a tit-for-tat situation.

Diana and Hewitt met often at his mother's small cottage in Devon. "He said, 'I'd cook and she'd wash up. Just dinner and relaxing and laughing. We also enjoyed walking along the beach.'"

Hewitt, however, was not always entirely happy about being with Diana. Wharfe wrote that Hewitt sometimes tried to "escape" from her. Hewitt once told Wharfe, "When I need some time off, the Princess can be so demanding."

Paradoxically, Diana at this time still craved more in her life. She began to see Hewitt less and less. When he called to ask to meet, she began saying she was too busy with her work.

Wharfe wrote that Diana "seemed to ignore her own infidelity, but would explode at Charles' relationship [with Camilla]. She even thought the Queen sanctioned his adultery. Hypocrisy of this nature was her metier. In Diana's mind, perversely, there was no contradiction in her behavior, which gives an insight into her complex character."

Diana's affair with Hewitt was put on hold when he was assigned to active duty in the Gulf War in 1991 and he became a tank commander. Their relationship later resumed, but it was less intense. Diana told Wharfe that she never had been completely convinced that Hewitt's declarations of love were entirely genuine. He might just be attracted to the idea of snaring a princess who was the most famous woman in the world.

Shortly after Hewitt's return from the war, Diana phoned him saying it would be best if they "cooled things" for the time being.

Hewitt was then assigned to Germany for six months. When he returned to London, he discovered that Diana's love life had moved on. He blamed media attention to their affair for ending it. She openly blamed, according to Wharfe, "his stupidity."

Hewitt was always in need of money. While he and Diana were lovers, he admitted this and said he needed a new car, but didn't have the money to buy one. She paid for his new car.

Upon his return to London, she was perhaps paranoid and began to fear that Hewitt might try to blackmail her. His need for money from his relationship with her surfaced in another way.

Six months after he retired from the Army in 1994, a book was published that told a lot about Princess Diana's dalliances with other men while she was married to Prince Charles. She was very disheartened to learn that Hewitt was the source of much of the scandalous book, *Princess in Love* by Anna Pasternak.

Diana considered Hewitt's quotes in the book to be a serious betrayal of trust and her privacy. She broke off her affair with Hewitt, but the following year, a film was released based on the book which compounded Diana's resentment of Hewitt.

Diana asked Hewitt to return her 64 love letters to him, but he refused. In 2003, his girlfriend at the time allegedly stole the letters and tried to sell them to the *Daily Mirror* for the British equivalent of several million dollars. Its editor, Piers Morgan, declined and returned the letters to Diana's estate.

Diana's friend Sarah "Fergie" Ferguson, Duchess of York, blamed Hewitt, although there has been no proof he tried to sell the letters. Nonetheless, she condemned his action and said, "Betrayal, I think is the most horrible, horrible, disloyal thing you can do to anyone."

Ferguson married Prince Andrew, the Duke of York, second son of the Queen and Prince Philip, and Prince Charles's younger brother, in 1986. Their union was short-lived and they separated in 1992. Fergie, never liked by the royal family, soon found herself in a scandal. She was photographed in a compromising situation while on vacation with her financial advisor, John Bryan. The picture, which made front pages of tabloid newspapers and magazines, showed him sucking on her toes while her young daughters were standing nearby. Fergie was then banished from the royal family. She and Andrew divorced in 1996.

In 2019 Andrew was accused in a sensational sex-for-sale business involving teenage girls. He denies any involvement in the matter. It was allegedly run by billionaire Jeffrey Epstein who committed suicide in jail in 2019 while awaiting trial in the scandal.

Diana also considered Hewitt's quotes in the book to be a serious betrayal of trust and her privacy. She broke off her affair with Hewitt, but the following year, a film was released based on the book which compounded Diana's resentment of her former lover.

After Diana ended their affair, Hewitt considered suicide. He prepared for a trip to France and planned to shoot himself. He said later, "I got in my car and loaded a few things up to get on the ferry to go to France to shoot myself. Then my mother insisted on coming with me. If she hadn't, I would have probably shot myself. So I owe her my life, really."

Hewitt opened a golf driving range in 1994. After that failed, he opened a bar in Marbella, Spain in 2009, but it closed after four years. In 2004, he was drunk when arrested for possession of cocaine. He died of heart trouble in 2017.

Rumors circulated before Diana's death that Hewitt was the real birth father of her son, Prince Harry. This was partly because both had red hair. Hewitt insisted he was not Harry's father. Diana was furious about the allegation and said red hair ran in the Spencer family.

9

Oliver Hoare

Oliver Hoare was an English art dealer who was another man with whom Diana had an affair during and after her marriage to Prince Charles. She confided in a friend, Lady Elsa Bowker, that she was "obsessed" with Hoare and dreamed of living with him in Italy.

Hoare was married and had three children. In 1976, he had married Diane de Waldner de Fruendstein who came from a wealthy French oil family. Her mother was a baroness, a niece of Queen Mother Mary.

Hoare was a friend of Prince Charles through their mutual interest in Iranian art and antiques. Diana met him when Charles invited Hoare and his wife to Windsor Castle in 1986. Darkly handsome, with thick, wavy black hair that he wore quite long, Diana became immediately attracted to him. Her father had died and Hoare, sixteen years older than she, may have become a father figure to her.

Ken Wharfe wrote that Diana had felt rejected by Prince Charles after the birth of Harry and felt drawn to Hoare. She believed that he possessed the strength and sophistication of a true man. Wharfe said Diana adored Hoare. "She craved him; she needed him at every conceivable moment."

Diana and Hoare met at friends' safe houses and Wharfe kept a "respectable" distance.

Diana's and Hoare's affair was so secret, she would sneak him into Kensington Palace in the trunk of her car. She had an apartment in the palace after her divorce from Prince Charles.

One early morning, while Prince Charles was away, Hoare was visiting Diana in her apartment, smoke alarms sounded. Wharfe wrote in his book "I ran out of my room and headed straight for the Princess's. But before I reached it, there, beside a huge potted palm tree in the hallway stood Hoare, [*nearly naked*], smoking a cigar. Diana, who hated the smell of smoke, had obviously told him to smoke in the hallway."

The next morning, Wharfe suggested jokingly to Diana that Hoare had perhaps been out in the hall in just his shorts because they had been playing strip poker. The Princess's face flushed, but she was not amused. Wharfe sensed that she would soon dispense with his services as a bodyguard.

Wharfe wrote that after she and Prince Charles separated, her fascination with Hoare intensified. "She had made him [*Hoare*] the center of her world, and in return she demanded his complete attention."

Wharfe did not think Diana's relationship with Hoare was a good idea and cautioned her to be careful or the media might discover them as lovers. Diana hounded Hoare with several hundred phone calls to his home. Hoare's wife answered many of the calls. When she heard Diana's voice, she hung up. Finally Mrs. Hoare had enough and in October 1993 she called the police about the nuisance calls.

Police traced the calls to Kensington Palace. Wharfe was questioned since he was Diana's bodyguard. He reluctantly said Diana must be the frequent caller, and told of her relationship with Hoare. Wharfe said he felt he had betrayed Diana, but had no recourse. He let the cat out of the bag because he feared one or more innocent member of her staff might have been blamed as the caller.

The media made front page headlines of the scandal. Diana felt that it was the last straw with the media. The expose also ended her affair with Hoare. It also ended Wharfe's job protecting the Princess.

Wharfe wrote in his book, "This, I am sure, led to her decision to do without police protection; a decision which I truly believe resulted in her death."

10

Theodore Forstmann

Diana's lovers didn't have to be handsome, but it helped if they were rich. Theodore Forstmann, a billionaire entrepreneur, fit that bill. He met Diana at a black-tie dinner in 1994. He then sent her flowers every week for three years.

Forstmann was an American-born founding partner of Forstmann & Little Company, a private equity firm in London. He also was CEO of IMG, a global sports and media company.

He never married, but adopted two boys in South Africa. He became romantically involved with Diana between 1994 and 1955, but almost nothing has been learned to describe details of their relationship.

U.S. Intelligence agents reportedly bugged Fortmann's phone calls with Diana. British agents also monitored their relationship. They denied her and her sons a permit to visit him abroad.

Forstmann ended his romance with Diana to resume a relationship with a former girlfriend. He died of brain cancer in 2011. He remains one of the main mystery men in Princess Diana's love life.

11

John F. Kennedy, Jr.

Did Princess Diana have an affair with John F. Kennedy, son of President Kennedy? Yes, says Simone Simmons, her "energy healer." She said Diana told her she had "a moment of true lust" with him when he was a magazine publisher in 1995.

Diana allegedly told her, "We started talking and one thing led to another and we ended up in bed together."

However, Diana's former butler Paul Burrell said it never happened and it is "a fictional story." But he added that if it happened, "It was just a one-night stand."

Kennedy Jr. had been a lawyer and then publisher of *George,* a magazine he launched in 1995. He edited it over the next four years until his death in a plane crash in 1999 at the age of 38.

12

Will Carling

Princess Diana was in a relationship with English rugby star Will Carling in 1995.

He met Diana after he had just married television host Julia Carling. Diana, then married to Prince Charles, had asked Carling to give her private fitness lessons. She then began to take her sons to his rugby matches.

Carling denied he was in a romantic relationship with Diana, but the media linked them together. After only a few months of marriage, rumors of the romance caused Carling's wife to divorce him.

Said Mrs. Carling, "I am mad that Will put himself in that position, and Princess did as well. This has happened to her before, and you hope she won't do these things again, but obviously she does."

13

Hasnat Khan

Diana called him "Mister Wonderful." Her friends said he was "The love of her life."

He is Hasnat Khan, a Pakistan-English heart surgeon. He and Princess Diana were in a secret romantic relationship from their first meeting in the late summer of 1995 to June 1997 when she broke off their relationship two months before her death.

The end of their romance was because he maintained that because of her public image, marriage with her was impossible. Their break-up broke Diana's heart and she continued to love him even on the night she died.

Khan was neither handsome nor rich, two qualities Diana loved in a man. What she saw in him was unlike what she had seen in any other man with whom she had been in a romantic relationship. Khan was her hope of returning to a normal life after being a front page public princess.

What did they have in common? Obviously, Diana and Khan were strongly physically attracted to each other. Her friends did not think he was good-looking, but physical beauty often lies in just the eyes of the person who loves them.

In the Muslim faith, both boys and girls are named Hasnat. In Arabic the name means "beautiful, fair, elegant, wise."

Diana and Hasnat had some similar sensibilities. Perhaps one thing that drew them to each other was they shared a mutual need to engage in humanitarianism. She had a strong emotional attraction to helping people, while he had the same to healing people.

Hasnat Khan was born on April 1, 1958 in Jhelum, a city in the Punjab province of Pakistan, the eldest of four children. His father, Rashid Khan, was a graduate of the London School of Economics who ran a prosperous glass factory.

After achieving a medical education specializing in heart and lung surgery, Khan worked at a hospital in Sydney, Australia and headed a cardiac hospital in Malaysia. In 2013 he began residency as a consultant cardio thoracic surgeon at Basildon University Hospital east of London.

Diana first saw Hasnat Khan on a September day in 1995 when he was in residence at London's royal Brompton Hospital. She went there to visit the husband of a friend who was recovering from heart surgery. Khan had assisted in the triple-bypass operation.

Diana was instantly attracted to Khan, seeing him in a hospital elevator, according to an article in *Vanity Fair*. She whispered to her friend, Oonagh Toffolo, "Isn't he drop-dead gorgeous?" Toffolo didn't think so, but didn't say so.

Diana later told Simone Simmons, her energy healer, that when her and Hasnat's eyes locked on each other, she told herself "I think I've met my Mister Wonderful."

Diana described Hasnat to Simmons: "He has dark-brown velvet eyes that you could just sink into."

Diana did not meet Khan that day, but returned the following day to look him up. In a *Guardian* article, she is said to have gone to the hospital "almost every day for three weeks to pursue him."

Diana's former butler, Paul Burrell, said years later that he wondered why Diana had been attracted to the doctor. In the ABC News special, *The Last 100 Days of Diana*, Burrell said, "He's the most unlikely character to be a lover for the princess. He's not sporty, he's not handsome, he's not wealthy, so what is it?"

One of Diana's friends told *Vanity Fair*, "When you think of the kind of men Diana must have met or been with or seen, here is a man who is completely and totally selfless. She said she never met anybody like him."

Diana finally was introduced to Hasnat, but it took two weeks, until mid-September, until he asked her out for the first time.

That came in the form of a visit to his Aunt Jane and Uncle Omar's house in Stafford-upon-Avon, to pick up some books.

Hasnat later said, "I did not think for one minute that she would say yes, but I asked her if she would like to come with me. I was very surprised when she said she would." After the visit, they had dinner together, then drove back to London. He said, "After this, our friendship turned into a relationship."

Diana delighted in how normal his life was. After years in the public eye, she had begun to crave normalcy. When he took her to a pub, she wanted to order the drinks because she had never had the chance to do that before.

Said Hasnat, "There wasn't any hierarchy in our relationship. She wasn't a princess and I wasn't a doctor."

Hasnat never spoke to anyone about the emotional aspects of their relationship, merely saying "she was very down-to-earth and she made everyone feel at ease." As for Diana's feelings for Hasnat, Burrell said Khan was "the true love of her life."

Hasnat was very uncomfortable with Diana's celebrity and she respected his privacy. To keep her growing relationship with him secret from those at the hospital, she would leave telephone messages using the name "Doctor Armani."

When they went out together, she sometimes disguised herself with a black wig and dark sunglasses so photographers would not recognize her. The need to disguise herself made Hasnat uncomfortable.

Tina Brown wrote in *The Diana Chronicles* that "Khan, hidden under a blanket in Paul Burrell's car, would arrive at Kensington Palace [*where Diana had an apartment*] with Kentucky Fried Chicken for dinner *a deux* with the princess."

Hospital staff did learn that Princess Diana was seeing Hasnat Khan there. In November 1995, Diana, as a joke, sent a huge flower arrangement to him, without a card. Someone called the florist and learned that the flowers had been ordered from Kensington Palace. After that, Diana was seen on visits to him at night in the hospital.

Hasnat did not want any part of the public world Diana lived in, constantly besieged by photographers. He said at the 2004 inquest into her death, "I told her that the only way I could see us having a vaguely normal life together would be if we went to Pakistan, as the press don't bother you there." He added, "I did not want to have to look over my shoulder all the time."

Jemima Khan, the wife of one of Hasnat's cousins, told *Vanity Fair* that Diana was "madly in love" with Hasnat Khan and "wanted to marry him, even if that meant living in Pakistan."

Diana made trips to Pakistan to meet with Hasnat's mother, sisters, and other family members, to try to win their support for her marriage to him. His strict Muslim mother strongly opposed it.

Hasnat also said at the inquest that he believed the car crash that took Diana's life had been a tragic accident. Also at the inquest, he told police that he doubted Diana had been pregnant when she died, because she always took her contraceptive pills.

Hasnat talked to Diana about the possibility of them getting married. He told her he would find the inevitable media attention "hell." He later told police at the inquest into her death, "My main concern about us getting married was that my life would be hell because of who she was. I knew I would not be able to live a normal life, and if we ever had children together, I would not be able to take them anywhere or do normal things with them."

Tina Brown wrote in her book, "I think Hasnat was very much in love with Diana, but had really reached the end of his tether because Diana pushed him and pushed him and pushed him to go public and say 'We're a couple,' and he wouldn't. So she gave him an ultimatum, "Either we go public or this isn't going to happen [*their relationship would end*]."

Hasnat rejected the ultimatum. He later said, "Even after two years, the relationship wasn't leading to a meaningful progression or conclusion, and that was the main stress on both of us."

Diana ended her relationship with Hasnat Khan in June 1997. She soon began one with wealthy playboy Dodi Fayed. It was said that she intentionally was photographed with him so as to make Hasnat jealous. He was said to have seen it differently.

He told a friend, "I think she wanted to be with someone who was happy to be seen with her in public, and she could do that with Dodi. I think she realized that he could give her all the things I could not."

Hasnat tried to reach Diana the night she died, but was unable to get through to her. Richard Kay, a friend of Diana's, wrote in *The Last 100 Days of Diana*, "I think he was worried about her, as were a lot of her friends, about what she'd gotten herself into [*with Muslim Fayed*]."

Hasnat revealed as much in a conversation later with Diana's friend Richard Kay. "He said to me, 'Maybe later in the summer, we'd have got back together again.'"

Paul Burrell speculated as to what Hasnat Khan would have said to Diana if he had been able to reach her by phone that fatal night. "I think Hasnat's last call would've said, 'Isn't it about time you come home to me? Because I miss you.'"

Burrell said he believed that had Diana returned to London the day after what became the last day of her life, Hasnat would have rekindled their romance. "They were true soul mates," he said.

Hasnat attended Diana's funeral. He married a Pakistani woman, Hadia Sher Ali, in an arranged marriage in 2006. They divorced after just 18 months. He remains single at this writing in 2019 and is a consultant cardiac surgeon at Basildon and Thurrock University Hospital in England.

14

Dodi Fayed

D odi Fayed, a billionaire Muslim Egyptian playboy, followed Hasnat Khan in Princess Diana's last romantic relationship.

Born Emad El-Din Muhamed Abdel Mena'em Fayed on April 15, 1955 in Alexandria, Egypt, he was commonly known as Dodi Fayed. His father was billionaire Mohamed El Fayed who had owned Harold's department store in London and the Hotel Ritz in Paris. After university he served as an attache at the United Arab Emirates Embassy in London. He also was a producer of "Chariots of Fire" and other films, and a creative consultant on the "F/X" television series.

They met in 1987, but didn't enter into a romantic relationship until ten years later. Their affair did not become newspaper and magazine front pages until the month they met, August 1997. They died together in the auto crash in Paris on August 31 that year.

Diana began her affair with Dodi in July 1997 as her two-year relationship began to come to an end with Khan, a Pakistani-English heart surgeon. After vacationing on Fayed's family yacht on the French and Italian Rivieras in August, they dined in Paris at the Ritz Hotel. Leaving the hotel early on the morning of August 31, they were hounded by paparazzi (photographers).

A fast-speed motor chase followed in the Pont de l'Alma tunnel and Diana's chauffeur Henri Paul turned the wheel of her limousine to avoid hitting another car. The limousine crashed into a pillar and Dodi and the chauffeur died instantly. Diana, taken to a nearby hospital, died two hours later of multiple injuries.

Prince Charles was with his sons at Balmoral Castle when he learned of Diana's death. He immediately arranged for a flight to Paris, leaving the boys there to be comforted by their grandmother, the Queen.

Diana's friend Paul Burrell who had known her since she was eighteen, was in London when he learned of Diana's death. He took a plane to Paris and got there before Charles. He went to the hospital and sat with Diana's body, holding her hand. Not wanting to believe she was dead, he beseeched her, "Wake up. You're asleep, aren't you?" He said he felt her spirit was there, watching and hearing him.

Paris police investigated the crash and determined that it had been caused by Paul because he had been intoxicated and on medication for depression.

Fayed's father claimed that his son and Diana were the victims of a planned death, saying they "were executed by MI6 [*British Intelligence*] agents." Fayed's father maintained that Diana had become trouble for the Queen and the British government. She had become beloved by the people and might have married his son, and her eldest son might become King, his step-father being a Muslim.

The couple had become engaged before their death, according to a Fayed family spokesman, Michael Cole. However, this may not have been true, because Diana had said she did not intend to marry Fayed.

Princess Diana apparently was still in love with Hasnat Khan at the time of her death. Whether they married or not, she would always have his love.

Now meet three men who were not Diana's lovers, but they were her friends and confidants and knew a lot about who she was.

15

Paul Burrell

Paul Burrell is a former servant of the British royal household. He was married and no romantic relationship with Princess Diana, but knew a lot about her, which we know through his comments and writing. He reportedly was her closest confidant and keeper of her secrets. He sold his recollections of the princess to the London *Daily Mirror* in 2002 for a large sum of money.

Burrell, whose father was a truck driver, began royal service as a Buckingham Palace footman at the age of 18. He became Queen Elizabeth II's footman a year later. In 1987 he joined the household of Prince Charles and Princess Diana at their home at Highgrove where he worked as her butler until her death in 1997. In 2001, he opened a florist shop in Farndon. Cheshire.

He met Maria Cosgrove, who had worked for Prince Philip, Duke of Edinburgh while they were working in Buckingham Palace. They married in 1983 and had two children together. They divorced in 2016 and a year later he announced he was marrying his male partner, Graham Cooper.

Burrell said that when Diana became Charles's wife and part of the royal family at Buckingham Palace, "She was thrown into the deep end and told to survive. She was never told how to survive, but she learned very quickly."

Burrell claimed that Diana described him as "the only man she ever trusted." Her mother, Frances Spencer Kydd, disputed that. She is said to have detested him and believed that he was "just another hanger-on grasping at Diana's celebrity."

Burrell said that when Diana was having an affair with Hasnat Khan, he had approached a Catholic priest about a private marriage between her and the Pakistani heart and lung surgeon. The marriage never took place. He called rumors that Diana planned to become engaged to Dodi Fayed "rubbish."

In 2003, Burrell released his memoir, *A royal Duty,* which describes his career as a servant of the royal Family and his time as butler to Prince Charles and Princess Diana at Highgrove, as well as his move to Diana's staff as butler at Buckingham Palace after her divorce from Prince Charles.

Burrell said the Queen Mother, Mary, did not like Diana after she married Prince Charles. He said he saw her one day walking through the study at Buckingham Palace and she paused when she saw a magazine with Diana's photo on the cover. She turned it over on its back and walked on.

Burrell said that meant to him that she and others of the royal family resented that she was outshining them. He thought "That was dangerous territory" for Diana.

Diana told Burrell there was a "ghost" in her marriage and that the ghost was Camilla Parker Bowles.

Burrell said when he was butler at Highgrove, Diana would call him to ask where Charles was. Charles was often there with Camilla, but Burrell would tell Diana he was out. Burrell said it was a very difficult balancing act to deal with them both.

One day the Prince found out he was talking to Diana and flew into a rage. "I hear you've had a conversation with my wife!" Charles said. "Why were you talking about me being out last night?" Burrell replied, "I'm sorry, sir, but you were." Charles snapped back, "Well, can't you lie about what you're bloody told?" Charles then picked up a book, stomped his foot, and threw the book across the room at Burrell. Burrell said Charles was "like a petulant child."

Diana became a fashion icon. But Burrell said Charles often criticized Diana about her clothes that were intentionally meant to lower her self-esteem. "I know one occasion she came downstairs wearing a beautiful black and white Catherine Walker gown. She asked, 'Do you like it?' He replied, 'You look like you belong in the Mafia.' That cut her down to her knees.

"Another time, she came down in a tartan dress. Again she asked, 'Do you like it?" He replied, 'You look like a Caledonian [airline] stewardess.' He was always under-rating her just before an engagement began, so she would lose her confidence. So it was mental cruelty, in a way. I never saw any physical cruelty. I saw tables being upset, I saw crockery being thrown across the room. But I never saw any physical violence."

"Another time, he told her 'When I married you, I made you a princess. You weren't born royal." This was a man born to be king. This was man who was treated from the very beginning like a God, suddenly being eclipsed by this woman. He wasn't very happy.

Diana told Burrell, "I kissed a frog. I found a toad." Her kiss had not turned it into Prince Charming. She found she had married Prince Uncharming. It was obvious to me, she had been a young naive girl."

Burrell said Charles told her before their separation, "I don't love you. I only married you to have a child, an heir." She then began to look for someone else to love her.

16

Ken Wharfe

"The Diana I knew was full of fun; almost always in search of laughter; not wallowing in self-pity and tears as she is now [after her death] so often portrayed."

That is how the princess is described by her bodyguard Ken Wharfe in his 2002 book *Diana: Closely Guarded Secret.*

"For nearly six years, from 1958 to 1993, I shadowed the late princess in my capacity as her Scotland Yard personal protection officer; her police bodyguard, during the most traumatic period of her life. For most of that time she was a joy to work with."

Wharfe guarded Diana every step of the way on her travels to Washington, D.C., India, the Caribbean, and Africa. Scotland Yard's code name for Diana was "Purple Five Two." Wharfe and Diana threw reporters and photographers off their trail by posing as man and wife, registering in hotels under the names Mr. and Mrs. Hargreaves.

At the same time Wharfe was bodyguard for Diana at her and Prince Charles's home at Highgrove, he was the same for their young sons, William and Harry. He wrote that they were typical fun-loving boys who often rough-housed together and got him to play ball games with them that exhausted him. The three of them became good friends over the years. Wharfe wrote that because of the prince's busy schedule, Charles was away from Highgrove a lot and, subsequently, he, Wharfe spent more time with the boys than their father did.

Wharfe wrote more about Diana: "Diana was an inveterate giggler, and when in that mood, the tiniest incident could send her into paroxysms of barely suppressed laughter. There were, of course, dark clouds in her life, but they would soon pass to allow her nature to shine brightly once again. Her name has been dragged through the mud, her principles derided, her motives corrupted, and even her sanity questioned. It has been, in my view at least, a vicious and one-sided war, and as in any war, the truth has been the first casualty."

Wharfe wrote that there are not many days he does not think of Diana. "Her illuminating smile, her sheer presence, and above all her yearning to live life to the full, have never left me."

He explained, "My intention in writing this book is simple... to set the record straight about the woman who herself once claimed that I knew her better than anyone, and in doing so, to tell the simple truth about one of the most remarkable, complex and alluring figures of the latter part of the twentieth century."

When the royal couple divorced, Wharfe took up the same bodyguard work for Diana who then had an apartment in Buckingham Palace. He wrote, "On paper, my job was simple... to keep her safe at all costs. This meant that either I or one of mt team would be on duty with her from the moment she got up to the moment she went to bed, without fail."

Regarding Diana's devotion to humanitarian work, spending a lot of time visiting sick children, the elderly, AIDS victims, homosexuals, and lepers, Wharfe wrote: "The word 'humanitarianism ' embodies the very essence of Diana. She believed that she could change humankind for the better. She tried; she raised our awareness [*to the needs of the sick and elderly.*]

Wharfe wrote:"Diana was not strong emotionally.... When she was alone [after taking a strong stand on a matter] her fortitude deserted her and, by her own account, she 'cried and cried and cried and didn't sleep that night.' Seeing her that evening, my heart went out to her, a young woman desperate to be wanted by the one man whom, I believe, she loved completely."

Prince Charles injured an arm but rejected Diana's wifely attempts to comfort him. Shortly afterward, their son William suffered a severe injury when a friend accidentally hit him in the head with a golf club. Charles and Diana went to the hospital but doctors said only one of them need remain as their son underwent surgery. Diana remained but Charles left and went to an opera. The incident made media headlines, one of which asked Charles, "What Kind of a Dad Are You?"

Charles then publicly humiliated Diana when both attended a party which Camilla also attended. Wharfe said that Diana took Camilla aside and privately but calmly confronted her rival by saying, "I'm sorry I'm in the way. I obviously am in the way and it must be hell for both of you, but I do know what is going on. Don't treat me like an idiot." Others at the party overheard and were titillated.

Diana decided not to kiss Camilla hello on the cheek anymore when they met.

"The incident was a terrible insult to Diana," Wharfe wrote, and that when they were back at Buckingham Palace later that night, Diana told Charles angrily, "How could you have done this to me? It was humiliating. How could you?"

Diana told Wharfe afterward, "Ken, there comes a time when you just don't care any more. That time has come." Wharfe wrote, "From the absolute calm of her manner, I knew that she meant it."

Wharfe then wrote about the "secret" in the title of his book, *Diana: Closely Guarded Secret.* "I knew that she wanted above all to escape her marriage, and to live a life in which she could be herself, something that she had often confided to me. What I did not know, however, was the one secret, in the years that I was with her, that she kept from me.

"Without my knowledge or that of almost anyone else close to her, the Princess had laid secret plans which she hoped would prove the 'no divorce' pundits wrong. The project was eventually to evolve into a book called *Diana: Her True Story,* and its publication would effectively bring her marriage to an end."

The book was first serialized in the *Sunday Times* starting on June 7, 1992. Diana took no prisoners in telling her story, which was about Charles' infidelity with Camilla but also told of her love affairs because her husband was unfaithful to her.

Charles then did a televised interview admitting his extra-marital affair with Camilla, without specifically naming her, and Diana followed with her own televised confession of infidelity. Millions of viewers all over the world were shocked, most of them siding with the Princess. It was too much for the Queen. She interviewed them together at the palace and insisted they divorce. Both reluctantly agreed.

Diana had gotten her wish. Her divorce. But be careful what you wish for.

And with the royal couple's divorce, Wharfe was out of a job.

Wharfe blamed Diana's death on her security team the night she died. He said that if he and his team were working with the Princess in 1997, they may have been able to prevent her death. But Scotland Yard had dismissed him from her service after her divorce.

Wharfe said, "On behalf of all the professional men and women of [Diana's] protection squad, let me say that neither [her bodyguard that night] Trever Rees-Jones nor any of the other bodyguards who attended Diana in the two months preceding her death were from our department."

Two months after Diana's death, Wharfe wrote to the Daily Mail: "I am still angry beyond words that this team of 'bodyguards' let her come to harm."

Rees-Jones and driver Henri Paul had been appointed by the Fayed family to protect Diana during her trip to Paris. Wharfe said Rees-Jones should have intervened when Dodi Fayed made risky decisions, like ordering Paul to drive although [Paul] allegedly been drinking. Fayed also should have told Paul not to engage in a high-speed chase to escape photographers. And Fayed should have called local police for back-up during the chase. Rees-Jones should also have insisted everyone in the car wear a seat belt.

"I can say with certainty," said Wharfe, "drawing on decades of police experience, that Diana's death was not murder but a dreadful accident that should have been avoided. She was not the victim of shadowy figures who regarded her as an embarrassment to the Establishment, but of her boyfriend's erratic behavior and her bodyguard's mistakes."

For his part, Rees-Jones told police that he had been unhappy with Fayed's plans that night, but "went along with it." Dodi's father blamed Rees-Jones for the crash, as did a police investigation.

After her divorce, Diana was on holiday in Cairo, Egypt in May 1992. Wharfe was there as her bodyguard when she asked him, in all seriousness,

"Ken, if anything happens to me, you'll let people know what I was really like, won't you?"

He did, in his book, as best as he knew her. He wrote that he hoped people would remember Diana as she was at her best, a fun-loving woman who, as she wished, really did make a difference.

17

Patrick Jephson

P atrick Jephson was Princess Diana's private secretary for seven years (1987 to 1996) during her marriage, separation, and divorce. He was often in discussions with her and her lawyers regarding those and other matters and contributed to decisions and speeches about them. He also traveled with Diana all over the world and they became good friends, but never lovers.

Jephson was another of Diana's friends who wrote controversial books about her during their years of service to her. His book, *Shadows of a Princess*, published in 2017, was uncomplimentary to Diana, and the royal family considered it to be another invasion of her privacy and another betrayal of the family.

Jephson described the atmosphere at Kensington Palace when he arrived in November 1991 to become Diana's private secretary as: "like watching a slowly spreading pool of blood seeping from under a locked door."

He also wrote, "The Princess could be a volatile, impatient young woman whose moods regularly swung from optimism to despair."

As it happened, one of the diciest things in Jephson's book was a quote from Diana herself. She said, about her jewelry, "They're a reward for years of purgatory for my f*****g years with this [the royal] family." She called her life with the royal family in Buckingham Palace "the dark ages."

PART THREE

The Inner Woman

1

Borderline Personality Disorder

B ritish author and journalist Ingrid Seward wrote about the royal family for 18 years. She took special notice of the relationship between Princess and the Queen, reporting on it in her 2001 book *The Queen and Di*.

Seward once asked Diana whether her marriage to Prince Charles had been arranged.

Diana replied emphatically, "It was Charles and I who decided on the marriage. Not the Queen. Us. No one else."

As the royal romance gained momentum, almost everyone urged the prince to press forward. But Prince Charles had some doubts about having proposed to Diana. Seward said he was confused. He told a friend, "I'm terrified sometimes of making a promise and then perhaps living to regret it."

Queen Elizabeth II never directly addressed the question of Charles' marriage. However, Seward said that by "nod and nuance," she made it clear she approved of Diana. Because Diana had become a royal as a teenager, the Queen reportedly was confident that 20-year-old Diana knew what would be expected of her as wife of the potential future king.

But the Queen was wrong. Diana didn't have a clue as to what the royal family expected of her. She was overwhelmed by the constant attention of the media. Even before her marriage, she lamented because she had lost her privacy.

The engagement was announced on February 24, 1981. Diana moved into a suite of rooms in Buckingham Palace. Worried about pleasing everyone in the palace, and heartbroken that Charles was still in love with Camilla Parker Bowles whom he was seeing both during his engagement to Diana. To relax, she often visited the palace kitchen to eat whatever she could find. Then she would throw up, so as not to gain weight. The eating disorder is called bulimia.

On her honeymoon and afterward, Diana was very sick with a bad case of nerves on top of her eating disorder. Diana's mood swings caused arguments between her and Charles.

The Queen overlooked the couple's marital problems, She believed that Diana would feel better as time passed and she became more at ease in the royal family and her role in it.

After the couple's honeymoon cruise in the Mediterranean, they returned to their home in Balmoral, Scotland. Diana saw Charles wearing a pair of cuff links with the letters "C" entwined. She assumed the letters were for Charles and Camilla, so she asked, "Camilla gave you those, didn't she?" He replied, "Yes, so what's wrong? They're a present from a friend." They had a row because of that.

More violent arguments became more frequent. Charles summoned the first of many doctors to learn what ailed the princess. She had eight sessions with a psychiatrist but they did not help her paranoia or depression. She was prescribed Valium to help her relax, but she didn't take it. Instead, she over-ate and developed bulimia.

Diana said, "All the analysts and psychiatrists you could ever dream of came plodding in to sort me out."

They diagnosed that Princess Diana suffered from Borderline Personality Disorder. Symptoms include fear of abandonment, a tendency toward histrionic behavior, a need for adoration, bulimia, and mood swings. That is a generic list for those with the malady, but they fit the Princess quite nicely, don't they?

Now that shrinks thought they knew what Diana's mental malady was, they gave her medication which didn't help her much if at all. What she needed was not tranquilizers but love and appreciation.

As the royal romance gained momentum, almost everyone urged the prince to press forward. But Prince Charles had some doubts about having proposed to Diana. Seward said he was confused. He told a friend, "I'm terrified sometimes of making a promise and then perhaps living to regret it." He was said to have cried the night before his wedding.

Seward wrote that the Queen gradually began to warm toward Diana as the Princess became pregnant with William. The monarch hoped that the baby would heal the wounds in the marriage. Diana felt that the Queen's support was a source of enormous comfort. "I have the best mother-in-law in the world, she told Seward.

Diana's pregnancy added yet anther stress as he hoped she would deliver a boy. Charles' much-desired heir. That certainly would please him and he would show some affection.

Through all these stresses during her marriage, as she increased her humanitarian work, Diana presented a captivating image of beauty, bravery, and compassion. Was it now a simple matter of doing what the old song says... "Make Someone Happy, and you will be happy, too." It was popular during her lifetime.

2

Diana's True Love

We learn more about Princess Diana's inner woman from Sally Bedell Smith in her 1999 book *Diana In Search of Herself.* Two years after Diana's death, Smith, a Washington-based biographer, portrayed her as infinitely more troubled than the public realized.

Though Diana radiated grace and poise, she suffered terribly from chronic loneliness and an overpowering insecurity. She hated being hounded by the press, but at the same time often initiated telephone calls to reporters.

"Diana was trapped in a terrible hall of mirrors," Smith wrote. "There was a huge disconnect between her public persona and her private life."

In a review of Smith's book in *People Weekly* magazine, we learn that Smith interviewed more than 150 people who knew the princess, including her closest friends, staff and advisers, some of whom had never before talked about her to reporters.

Smith wrote that people with Borderline Personality Disorder are "self-destructive, easily depressed, panicky, and volatile. But on the surface, they are apt to be charming, insightful, witty, and lively."

Smith also believed that Prince Charles "lacked the knowledge and temperament to help Diana deal with her torment." However, she wrote, "He probably deserves more credit than he has received for trying to get her into therapy" during their 15-year marriage.

Smith said that researching and writing her book was even more personally "unsettling" than she expected. "It is," she said, "the saddest project I've ever worked on. Diana needed so much help, and, due to her position and the nature of her problems, she was never able to get it."

Regarding Diana's many loves, Smith said one of the princess' close friends said "She was emotionally more stable when she was with [*Hasnat Khan*]. He taught her that she *could* be loved. " Diana had never believed that of herself.

Diana told friends that she was especially pleased that Hasnat admired her empathy for the sick. As Diana told her friend Elsa Bowker, "I found my peace. He [*Hasnat Khan*] has given me all the things I need" [Especially acceptance and true love].

Diana's love always tended to be possessive. This was also true in her relationship with Hasnat Khan, a Pakistan-British heart and lung surgeon. Smith wrote that "This time, she tried to advance Khan's career" [although he was already well-respected when she met him a few months before her death.] She asked South African heart surgery pioneer Dr. Christian Barnard if he could help find Khan a hospital post in South Africa. It could help financially if they married.

Diana had revealed that she loved Hasnat and wanted to marry him and "have a pair of girls." She wanted to move away from London and live with Hasnat in South Africa. It was her first choice for relocation because her brother Charles lived there.

Diana feared Hasnat would reject her, as many others she loved had, so,she tried to control him. Her energy healer, Simone Simmons, a kind of psychotherapist, recalled that Diana was "so impatient to have Hasnat's undivided attention that if he used the Kensington Palace [where she had an apartment] telephones to speak to his family or friends in Pakistan for more than ten minutes, Diana would turn her music up or dance before him to distract his attention." She also frequently telephoned Hasnat at the hospital and, Simmons said, "was often upset if he was in the operating theater and couldn't talk to her."

For nearly18 months Diana persistently misled the media about her affair with Hasnat Khan. Smith wrote that her motive for lying, saying they were just friends, was to protect him as she sought to make their relationship work.

"She would have converted to Islam, she would have done anything, [if he would marry her], said Elsa Bowker. But Diana miscalculated when she made a spur-of-the-moment visit to Pakistan in May1997. Her unstated purpose for the trip was to meet Hasnat's family and "convince them that she was a nice girl" and worthy of becoming his wife.

On her visit to Pakistan, Diana wore a traditional shalwar kameez [trousers and long shirt or tunic]. She spent 90 minutes with a dozen of Khan's relatives, including his parents and grandmother. She failed to convince them that Hasnat should marry her.

Upon her return to London a few days later, Diana told friends she had made a good impression on Hasnat's family and that her marriage to him was now possible. But he was dismayed that she had not told him she was going to see his family in Pakistan. He also rebuked her for revealing it to the press. It brought their relationship into the open, which he was greatly opposed to.

A week later, *Hello!* magazine reported that Hasnat's father had expressed doubts that Hasnat and Diana would marry. Their relationship went further into secrecy. Her friend, historian Paul Johnson, said of this time, "She said he [*Hasnat*] was more afraid of his family and religion and background than he was in love with her."

An article in the *Sunday Mirror* tabloid in July reported that Diana and Khan had become "unofficially engaged" after the "amazing summit meeting" with his family in Pakistan. Khan accused Diana of leaking the story, although she denied it and was "very sore and hurting." The false report caused Khan to then break off his relationship with her. He told her he couldn't live with the pressure of the media coverage of their relationship. Diana's friend Simmons said that the morning after the break-up, Diana "was sobbing her heart out."

Diana then went on vacation with her sons to the south of France to be with playboy Dodi Fayed. She resided in the home of his father at Saint-Tropez, a beautiful French Riviera town famous for its nudist beaches. His role in bribing members of the British Parliament for financial favors was back in the news at the time.

Diana spent time with Dodi on his father's yacht. Smith wrote about Dodi: "He was emotionally immature. And he wasn't very bright. But like Diana, he had been abandoned [*by his mother when he was a boy, as Diana had been by her mother*]. They were both looking for something missing in themselves."

Diana and her sons returned to Kensington Palace in London on July 20. Dodi sent pink roses to her that filled the apartment. He also showered her with gifts including an $11,000 gold watch. His father sent her a large box of fruit. She told a friend, astrologer Debbie Frank, about her trip. She said she had "the best holiday I've ever had. I've met someone."

Diana was off to Paris with Dodi on July 25. They secretly stayed at the Ritz Hotel which his father owned. Diana stayed without pay at the Imperial Suite which rented at $10,000 a night. Two days later they returned to London.

In late July, while her sons were at Balmoral, Diana and Dodi went on a six-day cruise off Sardinia and Corsica aboard his father's yacht. Their love affair reportedly began there.

Tabloids headlined the Diana-Dodi romance on August 7, the day they returned to London. She enjoyed having the romance splashed across the front pages of newspapers after having had to keep her romance with Hasnat Khan secret. She hoped he would see the articles and they would make him jealous so he would return to her. But it didn't work. Khan reportedly felt she had just found someone to replace him who relished having a public romance.

Dodi's friend Nora Summers said about Diana and Dodi,, "They were in many ways ill-fated and the perfect awful couple."

Diana and Dodi returned to Paris for romantic weekend on August 30. They drove in his Mercedes limousine to his apartment where they spent the night together.

Dodi eventually had become annoyed with paparazzi who pursued them everywhere. To avoid them at dinner in the Ritz, they ate in their suite at the hotel. Afterward, they left by a rear door and headed for a rented Mercedes. As Diana and Dodi got into the back seat, their chauffeur, Henri Paul, shouted to the paparazzi snapping photos of them, "Don't bother following... you won't catch us!"

The paparazzi took up the challenge and in a chase of less than fifteen minutes, Dodi and Paul were dead and Diana would die in hospital a few hours later.

Diana and Dodi Fayed had known each other for only six weeks. They were together on 32 of those days, but had been alone together only 25 of those days.

Smith wrote that in Diana's final summer, she sent out many conflicting signals, playing out in public her shifting moods, doubts and insecurities in exaggerated form. Her romance with Dodi may have been the clearest evidence that she had made little progress dealing with her demons.

"I work by instinct," Diana had said three months before she died. "It's my best adviser."

Smith assessed that because of the number of times her instinct failed her, it was a stark admission that Princess Diana had remained sadly out of touch with herself to the very end.

3

Diana and the Monarchy

Diana had told Stephen Twigg, her counselor, that she feared the British monarchy's future was in deep trouble. He said, "She finds the monarchy claustrophobic and completely outdated with no relevance to today's life and problems. She feels that it is a crumbling institution and believes that the royal family won't know what has hit it in a few years unless it changes."

What impact did Princess Diana have on the royal family and the British Empire?

Twenty-two years after her death, Princess Diana is remembered for having done more to transform the British monarchy than perhaps any other member of the royal family. From her charity work to her closeness to the common Briton, raising her sons to have empathy for the disadvantaged, and becoming "The People's Princess," captivating the world as a fashion icon, her legacy lives on.

Diana's reputation for working tirelessly on behalf of charitable causes has kept her in the hearts of people around the world. She remains extraordinary and irreplaceable, as her brother described her.

Diana's fearlessness and compassion led her to work on behalf of those she described as rejected by society: victims of HIV, AIDS, leprosy. Her showing no fear in taking the hand of AIDS patients had a global effect in eliminating the fear most people had in having any physical contact with victims of the disease.

She said, "Having HIV does not make people dangerous to know. You can shake their hands and give them a hug. Heaven knows they need it."

Diana's charity work expanded to include the Leprosy Mission in Great Britain, of which she became patron. Another of the causes she was most famously involved with was that of land mine removal, and she was photographed walking through an Angolan minefield wearing protective gear.

Her son Harry made headlines when in September 2019 he retraced her steps through a minefield in Huambo, Angola. He brought new attention to the tragedy of people losing limbs or their lives from exploding mines still buried from past wars.

Diana was not only a patron of more than 100 charities, she was an active patron. Today her charity work lives on in her sons. She had taught them to have empathy for the disadvantaged, and they have become active in bringing attention to mental health, homelessness, and HIV awareness.

Prime Minister Tony Blair said, about Diana's affect on the British monarchy, that she brought renewed attention to the question of the future of the monarchy. He said he sensed that Britons shared her belief that changes were needed in the monarchy, to make it less distant from the people and more caring. "Something must come of all this," he said.

"That monarchy [*as it was before Diana*] is over," said David Starkey, a leading British monarchy historian. "It's dead, and on its tombstone will be written: Died at the hands of Diana, Princess of Wales, 1997."

4

What Only Diana's Closest
Friends Knew About Her

Diana kept a lot about herself to herself. Although one of the most public figures, she was a true mystery woman to most of the world. She only revealed parts of herself to her best friends. Some of these insights into who she was follow here.

Diana had a pet name for her critics and those who hated her. She called them "velvet headbands." As she said once to a friend, "Oh, those velvet headbands are at it again." She coined the words referring to women whose dowdy style often included the outdated hair accessory. They were grown women who still dressed like school girls. They never changed. Diana had become a beautiful, stylish princess, and that threatened them.

Diana was not only an excellent swimmer, but an accomplished diver. She loved to swim laps in the pool at Buckingham Palace most every morning. She also was a physical fitness enthusiast, often having personal exercise coaches.

Diana and Princess Grace Kelly were friends. They met at Diana's and Charles's engagement reception at Goldsmiths' Hall in London on March 3, 1981. It was the royal couple's first evening out since their engagement had been announced.

Dozens of photographers' flashbulbs went off as she stepped out of a car upon her arrival with Charles. He had disapproved of the dress she wore, and had told her so, which immediately lowered her self-confidence. It was a black strapless taffeta gown he told her was inappropriate and too revealing. He told her that the only time a royal family woman wore all-black was at a funeral. Diana said in her secret videotapes that she was terrified she was doing everything wrong.

A writer later described Diana's entrance as "The greatest sexual theatre since Cinderella swapped her scuffed scullery clogs for clogs for glass slippers."

Diana said in her tapes, "I was big-chested back then."

As the evening progressed, Diana grew ever more unsure of herself. "It was a horrendous occasion," she said. "I didn't know whether your handbag should be in your left hand or your right hand."

At a Buckingham Palace reception afterward, Princess Grace Kelly could see Diana was upset and tried to comfort her. Diana said in her secret videotapes that she sensed Grace needed comforting herself. "There were troubled waters under her. I saw that."

Diana never forgot Kelly's kindness. In her videotapes, Diana recalled that Grace afterward took her into a ladies' room at Buckingham Palace for a chat that night. Diana told about Charles's love for another woman, pressure from the press, and her fear for the future. Diana broke into tears. Grace Kelly hugged her and warned, "Don't worry. It's only going to get a lot worse."

Grace Kelly, an Academy Award-winning actress, had given up her film career at its height in 1956 to marry Prince Rainier III of Monaco. It was not known at the time, but she reportedly paid the prince $2 million to marry her. It was his government's price tag for her to become a princess.

Ironically, 18 months after the two princesses met, like Diana, Grace Kelly died in a car crash, in 1982. Diana flew to Monaco against Charles's objection to attend Grace Kelly's funeral.

Diana's friends also knew she had a "public" wardrobe and a "private" wardrobe. She loved jersey dresses, but couldn't wear them in public early in her marriage to Prince Charles. She loved whimsical, patterned sweaters and felt comfortable in overalls and jeans. After her wedding, those casual clothes were retired from her wardrobe.

Diana watched her spending. She never went shopping without a notebook in which she recorded her purchases.

Diana did not like losing her title as Princess. She reportedly felt hurt when the Queen insisted she give up her royal title as a condition of her divorce from Charles.

Diana the Humanitarian. She was presented with the Humanitarian of the Year award from the United Cerebral Palsy of New York Foundation in 1995. Former U.S. Secretary of State Henry Kissinger presented her with the award, and she asked him about finding "purpose" in her life after she and Prince Charles had divorced. Kissinger advised her "not to do things that she was against, but things that she was *for*."

Diana and Sarah Ferguson had a falling out. They had been friends in their childhood and enjoyed doing pranks together when both were married to royal princes and had apartments in Buckingham Palace. Their friendship ended when Ferguson wrote a book, *My Story: Sarah, Duchess of York,* in which Ferguson revealed some things about Diana that Diana objected to. For one thing, Ferguson said she had come down with a case of plantar warts from wearing a pair of Diana's shoes. They had not spoken to each other for several months before Diana's death.

The Laughing Princess. Not many people know how funny Diana was. Her son Harry does. A few years after her death, Prince Harry described what his mother was like off-camera. "Behind closed doors, she was a loving mother, and an incredibly funny person. Some of her jokes about Dad were actually hilarious. All I can hear is her laugh in my head." She once told him, "You can be as naughty as you want, but just don't get caught. She was the naughtiest parent."

The Teddy Bear Princess. She kept hundreds of stuffed animals admirers sent her over the years, according to her butler Paul Burrell in his book, *The Way We Were: Remembering Diana.* He wrote that her apartment in Buckingham Palace after her divorce was full of teddy bears and other stuffed animal toys she was sent. "The sofa in her bedroom was filled with teddy bears and 'cuddly' toys."

What Diana ate. Diana used to sneak into the kitchen at Buckingham Palace and eat all the raisins off the top of rich, calorie-filled bread and butter pudding. But she was otherwise very careful about what she ate. When not suffering from bulimia, she stuck mainly to a carbohydrate-free diet of egg whites and poached chicken.

Diana's nose. She thought it was too big. It was only in her last years that she felt she looked her best, because she felt healthy and strong.

5

Conspiracy Theories

One of the strangest things about Diana's death is that ten months before the fatal crash, she claimed in a letter to a friend that Charles was planning a car accident for her. She said the reasoning was so that he could marry Camilla Parker Bowles.

Conspiracy theories into Princess Diana's death were investigated for several years under the code name "Operation Paget."

Diana gave the note to her butler, Paul Burrell, and asked him to keep it, "just in case" something happened. The complete accusation was not revealed until 2007.

Diana wrote, "I am sitting here at my desk today in October, longing for someone to hug me and encourage me to keep strong and hold my head high. This particular phase of my life is the most dangerous. [*Someone*] is planning 'an accident' in my car, brake failure and serious head injury in order to make the path clear for him to marry [*Camilla*]."

Burrell also later said that the media had taken too much stock on Diana's note, which had seemed to be a passing thought for her when she was feeling anxiety.

Rumors, mostly from Fayed's billionaire father, Mohammad Al Fayed, circulated after his son's and Diana's death in the car crash, that Diana was pregnant with Fayed's baby and that the couple planned to get engaged soon. Some claimed that the royal family did not want the mother of an heir to the British throne, Prince William, to be married to a Muslim,

Fayed. However, blood tests indicated that Diana was not pregnant at the time of her death.

Fayed's father claimed that Dodi's bodyguard Trevor Rees-Jones knew that the crash was premeditated but did nothing to stop it. Rees-Jones supposedly even agreed to cover up details after the fact because the British secret service threatened to kill him if he revealed their plot.

Rees-Jones reported to police that he did receive threatening phone calls and letters after the tragedy, but not from any government agents. He said he was not particularly concerned about them.

Some conspiracy theorists said the paparazzi chasing Diana in the fatal crash were in on a morbid scheme, hoping the chase would end as it did.

After her divorce, Diana had a restraining order issued against one photographer because she claimed he had crashed into her car during a photo chase and was using tactics "calculated to cause me harm." Many photographers who once had loved her resented her later attitude toward them and they subsequently no longer wished her well.

Another conspiracy theory involved a former MI6 British Intelligence officer, Richard Tomlinson. He reportedly spread a rumor that he had seen intelligence files for an assassination of a foreign politician in Paris that had an "eerie similarity" to Diana's deadly crash. This led to rumors that the driver, Henri Paul, was in on the scheme and was an MI6 informant.

Paul had been security manager at the Ritz hotel for a salary of $35,000 a year. However, there was $250,000 in his bank account at the time of his death. It was the supposition of conspiracy theorists that the extra money came from MI6 in payment for his part in killing Diana. The royal family allegedly put up the money to keep Diana from marrying Fayed, an Egyptian Muslim, and having his children.

Tomlinson happened to have been let go from MI6 for leaking secrets, and was famous for trying to ruin the organization's reputation. He also never used Paul's name in connection to the accident.

Official reports of the crash said that Diana's driver, Henri Paul, had been drunk behind the wheel. Some, however, claimed that was just a decoy. Conspiracy theorists claimed that the samples used in forensic tests on Paul actually belonged to someone else, a suicide victim, and were used to frame Paul. But toxicologists tested four different samples and all suggested that Paul's blood-alcohol levels were three times the legal limit in France, and there was nothing to suggest that the samples did not come from Paul's body.

In driving Diana and Fayed from the Ritz hotel, Paul was said to have taken a strange diversion past one expected turn. Some people suspect the entrance to a slip road most drivers would have taken was purposely blocked by MI6, forcing Paul to head into a tunnel instead. When the car was in the tunnel, a bright light supposedly flashed, blinding Paul. The bright light apparently came from the headlights of an oncoming car. Paul swerved the car to avoid a collision, and his car hit a pillar.

Conspiracy theorists believed the oncoming car was a white Fiat that had been driven by a paparazzi who also was a British secret service agent who played his part in the "arranged fatal crash."

Later investigation found that Diana's car would have been going too fast to go down that first slip-road regardless, so it is unlikely that Paul suddenly had to choose another path.

The rest of the eye-witness accounts of the crash did not conclude which other vehicles were at the scene. Some people claimed that they saw one motorcycle, while others said they saw six motorcycles, and still others said they saw a black car race away. Yet others remembered seeing a white one. In any case, a car driving by an accident without stopping, was not enough to warrant claims of foul play.

As if rumors that the British MI6 Intelligence had been involved in the fatal crash, conspiracy theorists added that the American government had a hand in Diana's death. The story went that the American CIA [*Central Intelligence Agency*] and the NSA [*National Security Agency*] were monitoring Diana's phone calls and had 39 documents related to her.

CIA officials admitted it did have 1,054 pages of information about Diana. However, they said none of those documents were related to the crash.

The ambulance carrying Princess Diana, who was still alive after the car crash, passed one hospital without stopping on its way to another hospital farther away from the scene of the crash. Critics claimed that seemed fishy, especially because she had been kept at the scene for so long.

While treating Diana on location before taking her to the more distant hospital, which was different from what Britons or Americans would expect, it was common practice in Paris. French paramedics would treat victims as much as they could before moving them, rather than getting to the hospital as soon as possible.

As for the first hospital the ambulance passed, the responding firemen knew it was not equipped to deal with Diana's injuries. A investigation report concluded that nothing could have been done to save Diana.

Some conspiracy theorists maintained that the surgeons who operated on her at the hospital where firemen had taken her deliberately let her die. In response, the doctors said that because of Diana's injuries, it had been impossible to save her life.

One of the most fascinating conspiracy theories comes from an American couple who witnessed the fatal crash. They said that the crash was no accident and because of what they saw that night, they feared for their lives.

Jack and Robin Firestone were on vacation in Paris. They were en route to their hotel, sitting in the back seat of a taxi that drove into the tunnel a few minutes after the crash. They saw two "formal" and "awkwardly" parked" cars that had stopped at the front of Princess Diana's wrecked Mercedes S280 limousine. It was only the next morning, reading about the crash in newspapers, they learned that the woman in the car was the princess.

Robin said that the morning after the crash she and her husband told a policeman about the two parked cars they had seen there. She said, "We went up to him and I said, 'Listen, we were in the tunnel last night and we need to talk to the police because there are things that we saw.' Without hesitation, the officer said 'They have enough witnesses. Don't worry about it.'"

"We were dumbfounded. One of the most famous women in the world is killed and [the police] don't want to speak to witnesses."

The Firestone's got the same response from French authorities they tried to talk to. They were not called to testify in the first inquest into Diana's death that was held in London in January 2007.

Months later it was ruled that an inquest would be held in front of a jury, and the Firestone's testified at that. Dodi Fayed's father was there and spoke to them. He told them he believed his son and Princess Diana both had been murdered.

The Firestone's met with Fayed's legal team later in New York. It was obvious to them that neither the French nor the British wanted to listen to the Firestone's testimony.

The inquest jury returned a verdict of "unlawful killing" by Diana's driver Henri Paul and the paparazzi who had pursued her that night.

Years later, Robin said, "We still live in fear because of what we saw and what we were told. I do not think Diana's death was an accident, and the action of the authorities makes me believe that to this day more than ever. The whole thing was an establishment thing.

"I hope that one day, as William and Harry grow older, that they want to take responsibility to find out what really happened to their mother."

Diana's bodyguard, Ken Wharfe, blamed her death on her security team the night she died. He said that if he and his team were working with the Princess in 1997, they may have been able to prevent her death. But Scotland Yard had dismissed him from her service after her divorce.

Wharfe said, "On behalf of all the professional men and women of [Diana's] protection squad, let me say that neither [her bodyguard that night] Trever Rees-Jones nor any of the other bodyguards who attended Diana in the two months preceding her death were from our department."

Two months after Diana's death, Wharfe wrote to the Daily Mail: "I am still angry beyond words that this team of 'bodyguards' let her come to harm."

Rees-Jones and driver Henri Paul had been appointed by the Fayed family to protect Diana during her trip to Paris. Wharfe said Rees-Jones should have intervened when Dodi Fayed made risky decisions, like ordering Paul to drive although [Paul] allegedly been drinking. Fayed also should have told Paul not to engage in a high-speed chase to escape photographers. And Fayed should have called local police for back-up during the chase. Rees-Jones should also have insisted everyone in the car wear a seat belt.

"I can say with certainty," said Wharfe, "drawing on decades of police experience, that Diana's death was not murder but a dreadful accident that should have been avoided. She was not the victim of shadowy figures who regarded her as an embarrassment to the Establishment, but of her boyfriend's erratic behavior and her bodyguard's mistakes."

For his part, Rees-Jones told police that he had been unhappy with Fayed's plans that night, but "went along with it." However, Dodi's father blamed Rees-Jones for the crash, as did the police.

Operation Paget concluded that all the 175 conspiracy theories into Princess Diana's death were entirely without foundation, and that all that had happened that night was an incredibly unfortunate accident. Still, theories involving her death persist.

The conspiracy theory went a giant and highly controversial step further in 2017. A dying British MI5 Intelligence agent, John Hopkins, admitted in a deathbed confession that he killed Princess Diana.

The 80-year-old said he had been tasked as a hit man for the British government and carried out 23 assassinations between 1973 and 1999. His job often involved discretely assassinating those who "posed a threat to national security."

Hopkins said he worked as part of a cell of operatives who were trusted to conduct political assassinations during a period he described as "when MI5 operated with less external oversight." Victims included politicians, journalists, activists, and union leaders.

Hopkins said Princess Diana was the only woman he ever killed. "She was the only target where the order came directly from the royal family."

When he was asked how he felt about taking the life of The People's Princess, he said he felt "ambivalent" about her death. He described Diana as "a beautiful, kind-hearted woman who had her life cut tragically short, but "she also was putting the British Crown at risk. The royal family had evidence she was planning to divorce Charles. She knew too many royal secrets, She had a huge grudge and she was going to go public with all sorts of wild claims.

"My boss [at MI5] told me she had to die. He had received orders directly from Prince Philip [the Queen's consort], and we had to make it look like an accident. I had never killed a woman before, much less a princess, but I obeyed orders. I did it for Queen and country."

Hopkins said the operation was run under strict control from Buckingham Palace in direct cooperation with the mainstream media. The high-level conspiracy involved collusion between the media and the Palace to "square their stories, make sure everyone was on the same page. It was a well-run operation. British journalists all answer to editors who answer to oligarchs who all want knighthoods from the crime family at Buckingham Palace. There is no free person in Britain. We got away with murder."

Hopkins said if he made his revelation earlier, he expected to be killed before he could die of natural causes, but didn't mind. He said if his admission to having killed Diana was ever investigated, which he doubted it would, it would take years and he would be long dead. His "cell" in her killing were already dead, so there would be no witnesses. His "boss" in the so-called assassination, died in the early 2005s. Prince Philip would never even be questioned about it all.

Dominic Lawson, *Sunday Telegraph* editor and a friend of Diana, said, "Drunk or sober, no chauffeur would travel over 100 miles an hour in a tunnel with a 30 miles an hour speed limit unless he was ordered to do so by his boss."

6

Diana's Funeral

P rincess Diana had telephoned her friend and reporter Richard Kay six hours before her death. He said she had "decided to radically change her life."

Kay later explained, saying, "Millions of women dreamed of changing places with her, but the princess I knew yearned for the ordinary routine of their lives. She would say, "They don't know how lucky they are."

Kay said Diana told him in that phone call that she was planning to return home in London at Kensington Palace the next day, after her Paris visit that night with Dodi Fayed. She was going to join her sons, who were spending the month with their father at Balmoral Castle in Scotland. She would complete her obligations to her charities, and then completely withdraw from her public life. She was looking forward to finally being able to live not as a celebrity but as a private person. Unfortunately, that was not to happen.

Upon learning of Diana's death, British Prime Minister Tony Blair told reporters, "We are a nation in Great Britain in a state of shock and in grief that is so deeply painful for us. She was a wonderful and warm human being, though her own life was often sadly touched by tragedy. She touched the world with joy and comfort.

"People everywhere kept faith with Princess Diana. They liked her. They loved her and regarded her as one of the people. She was the people's princess [*it was he who coined the name*], and that is how she will stay and how she will remain in our hearts and our memories forever."

Queen Elizabeth II and the rest of the royal family was criticized for not appearing to share in the public grieving immediately after Diana's death. Newspaper headlines pleaded with them to "show us you care." Responding to this, the Queen went on television the day before Diana's funeral and said,

"What I say to you now as your Queen and as a grandmother, I say from my heart. First, I want to pay tribute to Diana, myself. She was an exceptional and gifted human being. In good times and bad, she never lost her capacity to smile and laugh, to inspire others with her warmth and kindness. I admired and respected her for her energy and commitment to others, especially for her devotion to her two boys.

"No one who knew Diana will ever forget her. Millions of others who never met her, but felt they knew her, will remember her. I, for one, believe there are lessons to be drawn from her life and from the extraordinary and moving reaction to her death. I share in your determination to cherish her memory."

The Queen did not say she loved Diana, or even liked her, and it is doubtful that she did.

The world mourned for Princess Diana with a great outpouring of love and flowers. London florists sold nearly $45 million of flowers to her followers who placed ten thousand tons of bouquets and wreaths at the gates of Buckingham and Kensington Palaces. Thousands of her followers waited in lines for up to eight hours to lay flowers and sign condolence books at St. James's Palace where Diana's body rested in a private chapel. They chanted, proclaiming, "She was one of us."

A woman from New Zealand wrote in one of the condolence books, "Although I didn't know her and had never met her, I feel like I have lost a friend." Another grieving person wrote, "Your life had great meaning to me. Your happiness was important to me. I never wanted you to suffer." A third wrote, "Not since JFK [*assassinated U.S. President John F. Kennedy*] has the tragic public passing of a vibrant, charismatic life touched the world so deeply." A fourth wrote, "We loved the shadows of your shadowed heart."

Tina Brown said, "Princess Diana had charisma. She had this great accessibility in which she always made everyone she spoke to feel as if she was only connecting to them. She showed sympathy and empathy. She connected with people in a very human way."

The funeral of Diana, Princess of Wales, was held at Westminster Abbey, the burial place of British kings, Queens, authors, generals, statesmen, composers and other famous Brits, on the morning of September 6, 1997. A gun carriage drawn by six black horses carried the solid oak coffin, which was draped in the maroon and gold royal standard and topped by three white wreaths, bedecked with white lilies and roses. The flowers included tulips from Diana's son William; roses from son Harry, with a note he wrote saying Mummy;" and lilies from her brother.

Crowds of mourners standing twenty deep lined the streets as the funeral procession went on a four-mile journey from her home in Kensington Palace to Buckingham Palace. The Queen and members of the royal family stood outside the gates as the procession passed. At St. James's Palace, Prince Charles; his sons Princes William and Harry; his father, Prince Philip; and Diana's brother, Charles Spencer all began slowly walking a few steps behind the gun carriage and coffin. Following them were five representatives from each of the 110 charities that Diana had helped, including Red Cross volunteers, the homeless, orphans and their caregivers, hospice workers, and people with AIDS.

Two thousand mourners stood waiting for the procession when it reached Westminster Abbey. At her funeral, besides the royals and others mentioned above were her mother and sisters. Among the foreign dignitaries who attended the funeral were Hillary Clinton, Henry Kissinger, Queen Noor of Jordan, film stars Tom Cruise, Tom Hanks, Nicole Kidman, film producer Steven Spielberg, and opera tenor Luciano Pavarotti.

Diana's friend Elton John also attended. He adapted his song "Candle in the Wind," about Marilyn Monroe's death, to the memory of Princess Diana. He called it "Goodbye, England's Rose."

The Archbishop of Canterbury eulogized Diana saying, "We give thanks for those qualities and strengths that endeared her to us; for the vulnerability; for her radiant and vibrant personality; for her ability to communicate warmth and compassion; for her readiness to identify with those less fortunate in our nation and the world. She became a beacon of strength and a source of hope for so many."

An estimated 2.5 billion people all around the world watched the funeral on television, about half the people on Earth.

After the funeral service, the coffin was driven to the Spencer family estate at Althorp for a private interment. Princess Diana was buried on an island in the center of a small lake. Her grave was surrounded by trees that she and her sons had planted as saplings a few years before.

7

Diana's "Secret Daughter"

Perhaps the most bizarre allegation about Princess Diana was reported by writer Michael Thornton in the London *Daily Mail* in 2015. His article said that some claim that she had a baby daughter before giving birth to Prince William. The alleged "secret daughter" was said to now be grown up and living in the United States. It is most likely untrue, but the tabloid newspaper's editor insisted the article reported fact, not fiction.

The "secret daughter," named Sarah, was now 33 and reportedly said she was living in fear of being killed because of a law changing the succession to the British crown. Before 2013, the law of primogeniture was in effect in England whereby the first male born to a reigning Queen would succeed her as king. The Succession to the Crown Act of 2013 then allowed females the same priority in the succession as males. Sarah, and not Princes Charles or William, would be next in line to wear Queen Elizabeth II's crown and rule the British Empire.

Doubters of the Diana's Daughter story wondered how she could have given birth to a child before giving life to Prince William who was born in June, 1982, only 11 months after Diana and Charles married.

Those who claimed that the "secret daughter" exists responded by saying that in 1980, Lady Diana Spencer, then a 19-year-old virgin, was ordered by the Queen to undergo gynecological tests to establish that she was capable of bearing children before her engagement to the heir to the throne could be announced.

During these tests, it was alleged, Diana's eggs were harvested and fertilized with Prince Charles' sperm. The fertility tests were successful and the engagement of Charles and Diana was announced.

The story went that one of the team who examined Diana, a "rogue doctor," secretly held the embryos back and implanted it in his own wife. Unknown to the woman, she became the surrogate mother of the first biological child of the future king and Queen of England.

It is probably all preposterous and fiction, but the intention of the author of this book is to report all research he found on Princess Diana. The reader can take her so-called "secret daughter" allegation with a whole box of salt, much less a grain.

Sarah was reportedly born in October 1981, ten weeks after Diana and Charles were married on July 29 of that year, eight months before William's birth on June 21, 1982.

As she grew up, said Sarah, she was always told that she was a "dead ringer' for Princess Diana. When she was in her late 20s, her parents were both killed in a car accident. After their deaths, she is said to have come across a diary which revealed she had been born the product of a donated embryo and of *in vitro* fertilization.

Sarah is said to have tried to learn if the diary entry was true, but a threatening message on her telephone answering machine frightened her into stopping to learn who had really been her birth mother. The message warned her to stop looking if she valued her life. Learning that some believed Diana had been murdered in the car crash, and fearing for her own life, Sarah stopped her research and moved to the United States where she has lived under a secret identity.

Yet, the *Daily Mail* reported later a further chapter in the story of Diana's so-called "mystery daughter." Prince William and his wife, Kate Middleton, reportedly went to New York to check out the story and supposedly met Sarah. They reportedly said she was beautiful and looked just like Diana.

A witness to the 44-minute meeting said Sarah was "tall, elegant, and 'the spitting image' of Diana." She said "Sarah answered Kate's questions about her upbringing with apparent honesty."

Is Sarah an impostor, like Anna Anderson, the woman who claimed she was Grand Duchess Anastasia Romanov and the only survivor of the massacre of Russian Czar Nicholas and Empress Alexandra and their siblings in 1918 ?

Many believe that Sarah was a figment of the imagination based on the late Nancy E. Ryan's 2011 novel *The Disappearance of Olivia*, which in many ways parallels that of Princess Diana's "mystery daughter." In the book, Olivia Franklin, a young British pediatric physician, had been told all her life that she was the mirror image of Princess Diana. Her life is in danger as she searches for the truth of her identity.

8

In Her Own Words

Princess Diana said many profound things during her life, some of which follow:

"Everyone needs to be valued. Everyone has the potential to give something back."

"Carry out an act of random kindness, with no expectation of reward, safe in the knowledge that one day someone might do the same for you."

"Family is the most important thing in the world."

"Only do what your heart tells you."

"Everyone of us needs to show how much we care for each other, and in the process, care for ourselves."

"Life is just a journey."

"They say it is better to be poor and happy than rich and miserable, but how about a compromise like moderately rich and just moody?"

"Hugs can do a great amount of good; especially for children."

"If you find someone you love in your life, then hang on to that love."

"The greatest problem in the world today is intolerance. Everyone is so intolerant of each other."

"I don't want expensive gifts. I don't want to be bought. I have everything I want. I just want someone to be there for me, to make me feel safe and secure."

"I touch people. I think everyone needs that. Placing a hand on a friend's face means making contact."

"Helping people in need is a good and essential part of my life, a kind of destiny."

"Everywhere I see suffering, that is where I want to be, doing what I can."

"I'd like to be a Queen in people's hearts, but I don't see myself being Queen of this country."

"I don't go by the rule book. I lead from the heart, not the head."

"You can't comfort the afflicted with afflicting the comfortable."

"I think the biggest disease the world suffers from in this day and age is the disease of people feeling unloved. I know that I can give love for a minute, for half an hour, for a day, for a month, but I can give. I am very happy to do that. I want to do that."

"I live for my sons. I would be lost without them."

"I will fight for my children on any level so they can reach their fullest potential as human beings and in their public duties."

"I wear my heart on my sleeve."

"Call me Diana, not Princess Diana."

"My first thoughts are that I should not let people down, that I should support them and love them."

"Being a princess isn't all it's cracked up to be."

"I am not a political figure, I am a humanitarian figure. I always was, and always will be."

"It's vital that the monarchy keeps in touch with the people. It's what I try and do."

"The kindness and affection from the public have carried me through some of the most difficult periods, and always your love and affection have eased the journey."

"A mother's arms are more comforting than anyone else's."

"I think like any marriage, especially when you've had divorced parents like myself, you want to try even harder to make it work."

"I knew what my job was [*although no one told her*]. It was to go out and meet the people and love them."

"When you are happy, you can forgive a great deal."

"I like to be a free spirit. Some don't like that, but that's the way I am."

"Sadly, being royal is not always glamorous. To perform your royal duties, you need solid values to help you weather the ups and downs that come with the title."

Diana is quoted at the end of her book *Diana: Her True Story*, revised in 1997, saying: "I have learned much over the last years. From now on, I am going to own myself and be true to myself. I no longer want to live someone else's idea of what and who I am to be. I am going to be me."

9

Diana's "Pandora's Box"

Diana had been married to Prince Charles for 12 years when she gave sixteen private video and audio taped interviews with her speech coach Peter Settelen in her Kensington Palace apartment between September 1992 and December 1993. In the tapes she candidly told about her unhappy marriage and revealed shocking secret aspects of the royal family. Afterward, she kept the tapes hidden in a mahogany box she called her "Crown Jewels." Others later called it her "Pandora's Box" because the tapes revealed her highly sensitive reportage of royal family secrets.

Seven of the tapes became part of a BBC television documentary called "Diana: In Her Own Words," which aired in 2017.

Diana said that Prince Charles was given permission from his father Prince Philip to take on a mistress during his marriage to her.

Diana recalled going to the "top lady" [*the Queen*] for advice regarding her unhappy marriage, and sobbing. "I'm coming to you. What do I do?" The Queen said, "I don't know what you should do. Charles is hopeless."

"I didn't go back to her again for help," Diana said, "because I don't go back again if I don't get it the first time." [*Paul Burrell, Diana's butler, said the Queen "never interfered on any of her children's relationships. Her attitude is they make their own beds, they lie in them, and then they have to get on with it."*]

Diana said, "I remember saying to my husband, you know, why is this lady [*Camilla*] around?" He said, "Well, I refuse to be the only Prince of Wales who never had a mistress."

Diana also said, "My father-in-law [*Prince Philip*] said to my husband, 'Uh, if your marriage doesn't work out, you can always go back to her after five years."

Much of what else Diana said in the documentary appears in other chapters of this book.

The rest of the tapes – the more scandalous ones – together with photographs from Diana's personal collection, remain hidden somewhere, their contents never revealed.

We learn about the rest of the tapes from the 2019 book *Diana: Case Solved* by Dylan Howard and former detective Colin McLaren [*henceforth called H&M*]. They claim that the still-hidden tapes contain "a record of Diana's knowledge of scandals that could finish the British monarchy."

H&M wrote that after Diana's death, her sister, Sarah McCorquodale, and Diana's trusted butler, Paul Burrell, found a key hidden inside the cover of Diana's tennis racket in her Kensington Palace apartment. The key opened the mahogany box. Inside, they found the tapes, some letters, and a signet ring belonging to Diana's former lover James Hewitt.

The letters included several that H&M said were "vicious," sent to Diana from her father-in-law, Prince Philip.

More scandalous, wrote H&M, the box contained a photograph of Prince Charles "romping naked" with a male lover. They wrote that Michael Fawcett, Charles's former personal valet, had raped the Prince's former man-servant, George Anthony Smith. H&M wrote that according to Smith, Fawcett was Charles's gay lover, and he [*Smith*] had walked in on the Prince and Fawcett having sex together. If true, Charles was in a bisexual and not necessarily a gay relationship.

Smith, wrote H&M, told Diana about the rape when she visited him in hospital after Fawcett attacked him. It is not known who took the photograph of the Prince having sex with Fawcett, or how Diana came into possession of it.

It also is not known whether Sarah and Burrell watched the tapes before she gave the box and its contents to Burrell for safe-keeping. The box was later taken to the Spencer estate at Althorp where it supposedly is still hidden away.

H&M wrote that the royal family was "petrified" when they learned of the tapes and feared "their trail of affairs and seedy secrets coming out into the open. They wanted Diana out of the way."

H&M further wrote that Burrell was summoned to a three-hour meeting with the Queen at Buckingham Palace during which she "chillingly" told him that his life may be in danger from "knowing too much about the royal family."

10

Philip's Fatherly Advice

Prince Philip apparently took his own advice that he had given to his son Prince Charles about it being okay to have mistresses while being married. Rumors of Philip's philandering have persisted during his marriage to the Queen.

Sarah Bradford says in her book *Queen Elizabeth II: Her Life in Our Time*: "Prince Philip indeed enjoyed his fair share of affairs, and the Queen accepts it. He denies it, saying, 'How could I? I've had a detective in my company night and day since 1947,'" when he married the Queen.

Royal biographer Ingrid Seward said, "The Queen never looked at anyone else once she met Philip. He was just gorgeous. He was so handsome... tall, blond, and very funny." He might stray, "But he's always put his duty to the Queen first."

Seward, said Philip was rumored to have been in affairs with film actresses Merle Oberon and Anna Massey, singer Helene Cordet, Russian ballerina Galina Ulanova, and Daphne du Maurier, author of the novel *Rebecca*. Seward also wrote that Philip was in an affair with stage actress Pat Kirkwood, whose legs were called "the eighth wonder of the world," while Elizabeth was then a princess eight months pregnant with Prince Charles. Aside from the ladies, one journalist wrote that Philip "enjoyed a homosexual liaison" with former French President Valery Giscard d'Estaing.

When Prince Philip was a young man-about-town in 1947, he became a frequent member of The Thursday Club. It was a gentleman's-only club that held lively liquor lunches each week at Wheeler's oyster and seafood restaurant in central London's Soho district of night clubs and whore houses. The meetings were called "rip-roaring stag parties."

Philip earned the nickname "The Naked Waiter" when in his handsome and virile mid-twenties he served drinks at the club without his clothes, bare-chested and covering his royal jewels with only a small lace apron around his waist.

One wonders why he did that. Sometimes bartenders and waiters dress that way in gay bars and night clubs. Was Philip just joshing around teasing his club mates, some of whom may have had gay or bisexual tendencies? Homosexuality was against the law in Great Britain back then. LGBT rights for Britons were not legally protected until 1967.

Baron Nahum, a British photographer, founded The Thursday Club in 1947 with some newspaper editors and film actor James Robertson Justice. Philip became a member and was joined by David Miford Haven who had been best man at his wedding to the Queen, and also by his close ex-Navy friend and private secretary Michael Parker. So Philip went to Thursday Club meetings both before and during his marriage.

The club met at a time when women were the sexual playthings of powerful male members including actors David Niven and Peter Ustinov, writers including Arthur Koestler, photographer Cecil Beaton, aristocrats including Philip's cousin Marquess David Mountbatten, well-healed male members of upper-class British society, and even criminals and drug pushers. Larry Adler played the harmonica for them. They would gather and "frolic" in an upstairs room, away from the general public or their wives and girlfriends.

Gennady Sokolov wrote in his book *The Naked Spy [Mata Hari]* that a Russian billionaire, Boris Berezovsky, was murdered by British secret service agents, strangled with his own cashmere scarf, for threatening to release photographs of Prince Philip in a compromising situation with a young woman at The Thursday Club. A coroner's inquest merely concluded that Berezovsky was hanged but did not suggest he was murdered.

Typically, after a raucous lunch during which liquor flowed freely, The Thursday Club members gathered in David Mountbatten's apartment in Grosvenor Square. There, attractive young women including show girls and prostitutes joined the fun. They weren't there for stimulating conversation, but to service the men's sexual demands.

Eventually, The Thursday Club fizzled out. The owner of Wheeler's restaurant retired and the media had begun to publish articles about the club's sexual activities. Members became afraid they would be named in newspapers.

The Baltimore Sun alleged that as late as 1957 Philip was romantically involved with an unmarried woman he met regularly at the apartment of a society photographer.

The Queen accepted Philip's romantic adventures so long as he was discreet. Apparently he was not always discreet because biographers have written that into their ninth year of marriage, the royals separated for a time.

11

Diana and Mother Teresa

A strong spiritual friendship between Princess Diana and Mother Teresa, later Saint Teresa, began in India in February 1992. Diana and Charles were there on a diplomatic trip.

Diana was photographed sitting alone on a bench in front of the Taj Mahal, one of the world's most beautiful buildings and revered symbols to love. The ivory and white marble mausoleum on the south bank of the Yamuna river in the city of Agra had been commissioned in 1632 by the Mogul emperor Shah Jahan to house the tomb of his late beloved wife, Mumtal Mahal.

It was ironic that Diana sat there alone. Her husband, the man she still loved ["*whatever love means*"] despite his infidelity, was away attending a business meeting in Bangalore. Those who saw the photograph sensed that the royal couple was drifting apart. They would separate nine months later.

Diana visibly snubbed Charles later when he leaned over to kiss her cheek at a polo match in Jaipur. Observers said the attempted kiss was a second-thought by the Prince because he could see that photographers expected it, so he attempted to do his duty. The kiss would be profunct and there would be nothing personal in it.

Dickie Arbiter, a royal press officer, said that Diana was "incensed" and "swiveled so that the kiss landed near an ear. The crowd, as well as those of us accompanying the royal couple, could only cringe."

Diana's visit to India then took a major turn upward. She met nuns who worked for Mother Teresa, the octogenarian Roman Catholic nun who became an angel of care for the poor and sick of the country. Born in Albania, frail, 5-foot-tall Mother Teresa was active in humanitarianism work first in Ireland and then other countries but mainly in India. She founded Missionaries of Charity which now has 4,500 nuns working for the sick and poor in 133 countries.

Diana was visiting patients at the Mianpur Old Age Welfare Centre in Hyderbad on February 14, 1992. She met and shook hands with members of India's lowest class known as The Untouchables who were outcasts from society. It was unthinkable that a British princess would touch an Untouchable, but Diana did. The meeting was another example of Diana's fearless humanitarianism without regard for any criticism she might get from the royal family or the media. She did what she knew was right.

Diana showed touching compassion again on February 15 in Calcutta. She sat with a dying woman at Mother Teresa's Hospice and held her hand. Mother Teresa was not there at the time. Diana had a spiritual meeting with the future saint later, at Mother Teresa's convent in Rome, and found a "calling" in serving the needy.

Diana wrote to Paul Burrell, her butler back in London, that she had experienced a "spiritual awakening" in meeting Mother Teresa. It very likely changed the princess' life.

She wrote the letter to Burrell after visiting sick children in a hospital in India after meeting Mother Teresa. "Today," she wrote, "something very profound touched my life. I went to Mother Teresa's home and found the direction I've been searching for all these years.

"The sisters sang to me. They sang 'The Lord's Prayer,' and with our shoes off we prayed together on our knees.

"It was a deeply spiritual experience and I soared to such heights in my spirit. The light shone from within these ladies; saints, for want of a better word. Such love came from their eyes. I was then taken by Sister Frederica [*who came into*] the chapel to pray with the novices and sisters."

Diana became close friends with Mother Teresa, who was awarded the Nobel Peace Prize in 1979 for her humanitarian work, and was canonize a saint of the Roman Catholic Church in 2016. She and Diana died within days of each other; Diana on August 31, 1997, and Mother Teresa on September 5.

12

The Princess and the Queen

Diana loved to defy protocol, so it was inevitable that these two strong-willed women – Diana and her mother-in-law Queen Elizabeth II – would clash.

Their battle of wills reportedly broke the Queen's heart. It didn't help that Diana believed the Queen knew about Prince Charles' love for Camilla Parker Bowles and thought she even approved of it.

A confidant to the Queen said that at the start of the princess' marriage to Charles, "She [the Queen] felt the pretty girl was a misfit who didn't quite contribute to the things they [*the royal family*] did and they wanted her to do in the family. There was no real compatibility. Initially [*the Queen*] was sympathetic, but later on, I don't think she felt sorry for her; not really."

The Queen hadn't a clue as to why Diana visited those with AIDS, and that she even touched and hugged them. She told Diana, "Why can't you do something nice?" Nice would be to do anything not controversial.

For her part, Diana said she was "terrified" of the Queen. She felt that no matter what she did that might please her, the Queen criticized everything she did.

The Queen also was not happy that Diana was eclipsing her with the public. She wasn't used to sharing their love and loyalty; especially to a girl who seemed to be loved by the people because she touched them. Didn't she, the Queen, help the people survive World War II ? Diana had not even been born then, when she worked in the war effort in Army uniform by being a trained auto mechanic and truck driver?

As the royal couple's marriage was deteriorating, Diana talked to the Queen about Camilla and about Charles criticizing her so much, for her humanitarian work and her gowns which he never liked. Diana wept during most of the hour interview. Diana told the Queen she felt everyone in the palace was against her.

A lady-in-waiting to the Queen said, "She didn't know what to do." She always hated such confrontations, but distanced herself from most adversaries.

After the royal couple admitted their mutual infidelity, the Queen spoke to them about their marriage difficulties. Normally, the Queen did a good job of hiding her true feelings. She was seen by ladies-in-waiting as being heart-broken.

In 1992, Diana said in *Diana: Her True Story,* "The Queen thought my marital problems were caused by my bulimia." Diana considered her eating order to be a symptom, not the cause."

After Diana's death, the Queen's opinions of and feeling for the princess gradually improved. She had to agree Diana had contributed to the royal family. She often smiled as she watched her grandsons William and Harry play together. Silently, she knew to whom she owed them.

The confidant said, "She sees how much Diana radiates out of William and Harry and the effect they have on ordinary people. It is Diana that they see. That sense of fun; that easy way with people."

Queen Elizabeth II was heard to have said, with a smile, "Perhaps, after all, we have rather a lot to thank Diana for."

A sign of the times for a change in the royal family came recently, when Prince Harry, now grown and married, was seen leaving his car. He had opened the car door himself. The royals were not allowed to do anything physical; that was work for servants. Harry was late in opening his own car door. His wife had been seen opening a door a year earlier. Change was coming, albeit slowly. Both princes and their wives were bringing breaths of fresh air to the dusty monarchy.

Diana's legacy was/is alive and well.

13

Diana and Astrology

Diana had a strong belief in astrology. Born on July 1, 1961, her birth sign was Cancer [*those born June 21 to July 20*], and her ascending sign was Sagittarius. Her astrologer for many years was Debbie Frank, astrology columnist for the London *Daily Mail*. She was called "Astrologer to the Stars" because many of her clients were British and American film stars. Frank became part of Diana's "inner circle" of close friends.

Those born under the Zodiac sign of Cancer are "unflinching in the face of adversity." They know how to ride the waves of change and come out pretty unscathed. No problem is unsolvable. They may look hard on the outside, but are really soft inside. They are warm people; friendship and relationships are very important to them. They tend to put on weight when under stress. They can't stand to see people suffer, and will do all they can to help them. They have to be constantly reminded they are loved. These are typical characteristics of Cancers, but they apply remarkably to Princess Diana.

The key phrase associated with Cancer is "I feel."

Other famous people whose birth sign is Cancer include Nelson Mandela, equal rights activist; Helen Keller, blind and deaf humanitarian; and actors Meryl Streep, Errol Flynn, Harrison Ford, Katharine Hepburn, Tom Cruise, Tom Hanks, Sylvester Stallone, Robin Williams, and (*surprise?*) Camilla Parker Bowles (July 7, 1947).

Cancers consider sex to be one of the most sacred things on the planet. This may be another reason why Diana disliked Camilla Parker Bowles so much. Camilla seemed to be amused that she was able to play the love game with them.

One of her astrologers, Felix Lyle, said, "She is prone to depression, a woman who is easily defeated and dominated by those with a strong character. Diana has a self-destructive side. At any moment she could say 'to hell with the lot of you' and go off. The potential is there. She is a flower waiting to bud."

During one of Diana's astrology sessions, apparently in the months leading up to her death, she and Debbie Frank saw an eclipse of the sun on the horizon. Diana thought it meant a big change was coming in her life. Both thought it was a good omen. Good things were on the horizon for Diana.

14

William and Harry

Princess Diana's and Prince Charles's sons William (June 21, 1982 -) and Harry (September 15, 1984), are in any ways opposites. While William is more serious, Harry is more like his mother was, a mixture of serious and humorous mischief. Harry is more the "free spirit" than his brother, and has been criticized for that by the royal family, as Diana was. William has never been accused of acting less than royal, Harry has made tabloid headlines for night club partying and drinking, smoking marijuana, hitting a photographer in a fit of anger, and as a joke in bad taste, wearing a Nazi swastika armband at an observance of an Auschwitz concentration camp anniversary. Harry also was more athletic than William, especially at polo where Harry was fearless and William more cautious. William has been said to think before he leaps, weighing the consequences, while Harry leaps first.

Perhaps the brothers differ most in the relationship they had with their mother. Harry was a "mama's boy" and was said to be Diana's favorite. William also loved his mother but did not show it as much as Harry did. As a little boy, Harry would climb into Diana's bed in the morning and snuggle with her. Harry did not like sharing his mother's love with William and often told her, "I want you all to myself."

The brothers began something of a rift shortly after Harry married Meghan Markle in 2018. William and his wife Kate Middleton, who married a year before, lived in Kensington Palace, while Harry and

Meghan set up their royal home in the ten-bedroom Frogmore Cottage, a wedding gift from the Queen, on the grounds of Windsor Castle.

Following the separation of their royal households, rumors of tension between the brothers intensified after Harry and Meghan decided to cut ties with The Royal Foundation, a charity previously set up by the brothers to carry out their charitable projects. While the foundation continues on as before, William and Kate became solely in charge. Harry and Meghan reportedly wanted more freedom in choosing their charities.

15

"The Best Mother"

Princes William and Harry gave a television interview tribute to their mother in 2019. It was called "Diana, Our Mother: Her life and Legacy."

"Slowly, you try to rebuild your life," said William about the years after his mother's death. "You try to understand what happened. I kept myself busy, as well, to allow yourself to get through that initial shock phase. We're talking about as much as five to seven years afterwards."

Harry said, "If I'd known that that was the last time I would speak to my mother, the things that I would have said to her. All I do remember regretting for the rest of my life how short that phone call is. Looking back now, I have to live with that for the rest of my life."

On his future, Harry said, "All I want to do is make my mother incredibly proud. That's all I ever wanted to do."

On his wedding to Kate Middleton, William said, "When it came to the wedding, I felt that she [his mother] was there. You know, there was times when you look to someone or something for strength and I very much felt she was there for me."

Harry said about his mother. "She was our guardian, friend, and protector. She never once allowed her unfaltering love for us to go undemonstrative. Behind the media glare, to us, two children, she was quite simply the best mother in the world."

16

In Diana's Footsteps

As this is being written in 2020, Prince Harry and Princess Meghan, the British Duke and Duchess of Sussex, went on a two-week humanitarian pilgrimage in South Africa. They visited AIDS victims and walked the same landmine fields Diana went to in Angola a few months before her death to bring worldwide attention to the need to clear away the bombs that maimed or killed innocent survivors of warfare.

The royal couple met Sandra Thijika, an African woman who had a leg blown off by an exploding landmine in Angola when she was 13 years old. Princess Diana had met her and comforted her with a hug and held her hands. Harry and Meghan did the same for Sandra, now 35. She walked with a prosthetic leg and a metal cane on each arm.

Said Harry, "The meeting was deeply personal and meaningful to me."

They met at the Princess Diana Orthopedic Center in Angola. Diana had visited it in 1997 a few months before her death. It was since then renamed after her.

The royal couple said they planned to open a hospital in Angola in memory of his mother.

17

This Above All

M illions of Princess Diana's fans have visited her tomb on an island in a lake at her birthplace at Althorp. Others leave flowers at the iron gates at Kensington Palace where she lived after her divorce from Prince Charles. Many others around the world sent social media posts over Facebook and Twitter in tribute to her on August 29, 2019, the 22nd anniversary of her death.

One of the Internet posts Diana would really have liked seeing was that from the inmates of H.R.M. Prison in Dartmoor. They wrote: "Thank you for treating us like human beings, not criminals." The tribute was signed, "The Boys."

Princess Diana had been on a quest for love all her life, but the true love she searched for kept eluding her. After much trial and error, just about three months before her death, she believed she finally had found a man she truly loved and who loved her just as much. But even that love was not to be lasting.

Probably to Diana's surprise, her quest for real love did not end as she expected. Her complete fulfillment did not come from a man, not even from the two she most loved, cold and distant Prince Charles and warm Dr. Hasnat Khan.

Near the end of her life, Diana told a friend, author Kate Snell, "I'm no longer lonely. I know what love is now."

Snell said, "I think that's the gift one man gave her. And that man was Dr. Hasnat Khan." But Diana did not find lasting love even with Khan. She found it another way. To this above all Diana was true: she was true to her nature.

The love Diana finally found was in giving herself to others who needed the same compassion and affection for which she had been on a quest all her life. She loved giving herself with hand shakes and hugs.

Andrew Morton, in trying to sum up who Princess Diana was, said, "All through her life she was guided, not by argument or debate, but by instinct and intuition. It was a river which took her on a journey into the worlds of astrologers, psychics, soothsayers and therapists. Here lies the key that unlocks the doors between her personality and her universal appeal.

"This is why if Diana had lived forever, the media would never have understood or appreciated her. For she was not of their world nor did she share their values. When she looked at a rose, she savored its beauty, they counted the petals.

"She could be willful, exasperating, a flawed perfectionist who would disarm with a self-deprecating witticism, her penetrating cornflower blue eyes seduced with a glance. Her language knew no boundaries; her lexicon [*means of communication*] was that of the smile, the caress, the hug and the kiss, not the statement of the speech. She was endlessly fascinating and will remain eternally enigmatic."

Prince Charles, who told her he did not love her, sitting with his sons at Diana's funeral [*Camilla Parker Bowles was not there*] may not have understood Diana. More likely, Dr. Hasnat Khan, who told her he loved her, sitting unnoticed behind dark glasses, may have understood her sensibility better and felt that she finally had found peace.

As one mourner to Princess Diana's tomb said, "You were a Cinderella at the Ball. Now you are a Sleeping Beauty."

Neither the Queen nor Prince Philip attended the wedding ceremony of their son Prince Charles and Camilla Parker Bowles at Windsor Guildhall on April 9, 2005, conducted in the presence of others of the couple's families. It was followed by a Church of England Service of Prayer and Dedication, which incorporated an act of penitence, at St. George's Chapel, that the Queen and Philip did attend. They hosted a reception for the couple afterwards at Windsor Castle.

The Queen later said that Camilla Parker Bowles would never succeed her on the throne. Princess Diana and her rival but eventual friend Dale Tyron would have been glad to know that.

Good-night, sweet Princess. And may flights of angels sing thee to thy rest.

End

Works Consulted

Books

Andersen, Christopher, *The Day Diana Died*. New York: Random House, 1998.

Brown, Tina, *Remembering Diana*. Washington, D.C.: National Geographic, August 1, 2017.

Campbell, Lady Colin, *Diana in Private: The Princess Nobody Knows*. New York: St. Martin's, 1992.

Davies, Nicholas, *Diana: A Princess and Her Troubled Marriage*. New York: Birch Lane/Carol, 1992.

Dimbleby, Jonathan, *The Prince of Wales*. New York: Morrow, 1994.

Eade, Philip, *Prince Philip: The Turbulent Life of the Man Who Married Queen Elizabeth II*. New York: Harper Collins, 2011.

Holborn, Katy, *Princess Diana: The True Story of the People's Princess*. Amazon Digital Books, 2017.

Holden, Anthony, *Diana: Her Life and Her Legacy*. New York: Random House, 1997.

Howard, Dylan, with Colin McLaren, *Diana: Case Solved*: New York: Skyhorse, 2019.

Junor, Penny, *Diana: Princess of Wales.* Garden City, NY: Doubleday, 1983.

Lacey, Robert, *Princess.* New York: Times Books, 1982.

Morton, Andrew, *Diana: Her True Story.* New York: Simon & Schuster, 1997.

Oleksy, Walter, *Princess Diana.* San Diego: Lerner Books, 2000.

Rees-Jones, Trevor, *The Bodyguard's Story: Diana, the Crash and the Sole Survivor.* New York: Grand Central, 2000.

Seward, Ingrid, *Diana: An Intimate Portrait.* Chicago: Contemporary Books, 1988.

Simmons, Michael W., *The Life and Mission of Diana, Princess of Wales.* Create Space, 2017.

Smith, Sally Bedell, *Diana in Search of Herself.* New York: New York Times Books, 1999.

Spoto, Donald, *Diana: The Last Year.* New York: Harmony/Crown, 1997.

Whitaker, James, with Christopher Wilson, *Diana and Charles: Royal Blood Feud.* Graymalkin Media, 2018.

Periodicals

Chidley, Joe, "The Tabloid Princess," *Maclean's,* September 8, 1997.

Chua-Eoan, Howard, "In Living Memory," *Time,* September 15, 1997.

Green, Michelle, "Queen of Hearts," *People Weekly*,
    September 15, 1997.

Helliker, Sam, "How the Princess Lives On,"
    McCall's, December 1997.

Kay, Richard, "My Talk with Diana the Day
    She Died," McCall's, December 1997.

Television and Video Sources

ABC Television News, *Diana: Legacy of a Princess,*
    1961-1977. New York: MPI Home Video.

A&E Television, New York: *Biography*: "Diana:
    Her True Story, April 22-23, 1999.

A&E Television, New York: *Biography*: "Prince Charles,"
    June 24, 1994.

BBC, *Panorama,* Princess Diana Television Interview,
    November 20, 1995.

Diana: An Intimate Portrait, DVD, 2007.

The Private Life of Princess Diana, DVD, 2017

About the Author

Chicago-born Walter Oleksy is a journalism graduate of Michigan State University, a former reporter for the City News Bureau of Chicago, an investigative reporter and feature writer for *The Chicago Tribune*, and editor of three general interest national magazines. He has been freelancing for the past 40 years with that many books published, both fiction and nonfiction for adults, teenagers, and younger readers. One of his preteen novels, *If I'm Lost, How Come I Found You?*, was made into a two-part ABC Television After-school Special. His other books include *Lincoln's Unknown Private Life; Christmas with the Famous; The Murder-of-the-Month Club; Tomorrow; The Stolen Smile (a Mona Lisa mystery); A Midnight Clear: A Dog's Christmas; Clouds Over Pemberley*, a sequel to Jane Austen's *Pride and Prejudice, The Old Country Cookbook*, and biographies of James Dean, Christopher Reeve, Charlie Chaplin, Mikhail Gorbachev, a young adult biography of Princess Diana, and biographies of the sons of Abraham and Mary Todd Lincoln. His more than 100 magazine and newspaper feature articles have appeared in *Reader's Digest, Modern Maturity, Playboy* magazine, *The Chicago Tribune Sunday Magazine, The New York Times, The Los Angeles Times, The Chicago Tribune,* and the major travel and airline magazines. His writer's blog with a list of his books is at www.walteroleksybooks.com, and Amazon.com books. He lives in a Chicago suburb and welcomes e-mail at walteroleksy66@yahoo.com. A lifelong bachelor, he raised four adorable black Labrador Retrievers, one-at-a-time. He is currently writing a book about dogs, *Yes, Your Dog Loves You.*

CPSIA information can be obtained
at www.ICGtesting.com
Printed in the USA
BVHW031027181120
593415BV00021B/236